Read Real NIHONGO

Japanese texts
for intermediate learners

JN090578

Heart & Soul of the Japanese

にほんじん
日本人のこころ

Yamakuse Yoji

山久瀬洋二

Michael A. Cooney=translator

マイケル・クーニー＝訳

IBCパブリッシング

装　　幀 = 見増　勇介、関屋　晶子(ym design)
翻訳協力 = Matt Treyvaud

About the *Read Real NIHONGO* Series

Reading Sets You Free

The difficulty of reading Japanese is perhaps the greatest obstacle to the speedy mastery of the language. A highly motivated English speaker who wants to make rapid progress in a major European language such as Spanish, French or German need only acquire a grasp of the grammar and a smattering of vocabulary to become able to at least attempt to read a book. Thanks to a common alphabet, they can instantly identify every word on the page, locate them in a dictionary, and figure out—more or less—what is going on.

With Japanese, however, *kanji* ideograms make it infinitely harder to make the jump from reading with guidance from a teacher to reading freely by oneself. The chasm dividing the short example sentences of textbooks from the more intellectually rewarding world of real-world books and articles can appear unbridgeable. Japanese—to borrow Nassim Taleb's phrase—is an "Extremistan" language. *Either* you master two thousand *kanji* characters with their various readings to achieve breakthrough reading proficiency and the capacity for self-study *or* you fail to memorize enough *kanji*, your morale collapses, and you retire, tired of floating in a limbo of semi-literacy. At a certain point, Japanese is all or nothing, win or lose, put up or shut up.

The benefits of staying the course and acquiring the ability to read independently are, of course, enormous.

Firstly, acquiring the ability to study by yourself without needing a teacher increases the absolute number of hours that you can study from "classroom time only" to "as long as you want." If there is any truth to the theories about 10,000 hours of practice being needed to master any skill, then clearly the ability to log more hours of Japanese self-study has got to be a major competitive advantage.

Secondly, exposure to longer texts means that your Japanese input rises in simple quantitative terms. More Japanese *going into* your head means that, necessarily, more Japanese *stays in* your head! As well as retaining more words and idioms, you will also start to develop greater mental stamina. You will get accustomed to digesting Japanese in real-life "adult" portions rather than the child-sized portions you were used to in the classroom.

Thirdly, reading will help you develop tolerance for complexity as you start using context to help you figure things out for yourself. When reading a book, the process goes something like this: You read a sentence; should you fail to understand it first time, you read it again. Should it still not make sense to you, you can go onto the next sentence and use the meaning of that one to "reverse-engineer" the meaning of its predecessor, and so on. By doing this, you will become self-reliant, pragmatic and—this is significant—able to put up with gaps in your understanding without panicking, because you know they are only temporary. You will morph into a woodsman of language, able to live off the land, however it may be.

That is the main purpose of the *Read Real NIHONGO* series: to propel you across the chasm that separates those who read Japanese from those who cannot.

Furigana the Equalizer

Bilingual books have been popular in Japan since the 1990s. Over time, they have grown more sophisticated, adding features like comprehensive page-by-page glossaries, illustrations and online audio. What makes the *Read Real NIHONGO* series—a relative latecomer to the scene—special?

It all comes down to *furigana*. This is the first ever series of bilingual books to include *furigana* superscript above every single *kanji* word in the text. Commonly used in children's books in Japan, *furigana* is a tried-and-tested, non-intrusive and efficient way to learn to read *kanji* ideograms. By enabling you to decipher every word immediately, *furigana* helps you grasp the meaning of whole passages faster without needing to get bogged down in fruitless and demoralizing searches for the pronunciation of individual words.

By providing you with the pronunciation, *furigana* also enables you to commit new words to memory right away (since we remember more by sound than by appearance), as well as giving you the wherewithal to look them up, should you want to go beyond the single usage example on the facing English page. *Read Real NIHONGO* provides a mini-glossary on each right page to help you identify and commit to memory the most important words and phrases.

Raw Materials for Conversation

So much for *furigana* and the language-learning aspect—now for the content. The books in this series are all about Japan, from its customs, traditions and cuisine to its history, politics and economy. Providing essential insights into what makes the Japanese and their society tick, every book can help you as you transition from ignorant outsider to informed insider. The information the books contain gives you a treasure trove of raw materials you can use in conversations with Japanese people. Whether you want to amaze your interlocutors with your knowledge of Japanese religion, impress your work colleagues with your mastery of party-seating etiquette and correct bowing angles, or enjoy a heated discussion of the relative merits of arranged marriages versus love marriages, *Read Real NIHONGO* is very much the gift that keeps on giving.

We are confident that this series will help everyone—from students to businesspeople and diplomats to tourists—start reading Japanese painlessly while also learning about Japanese culture. Enjoy!

Tom Christian
Editor-in-Chief
Read Real NIHONGO Series

はじめに

　本書は、日本人が伝統的に抱き続けてきた価値観や思いをどのように英語で伝えるかということを、価値観を14のテーマに分類して、まとめたものです。

　文化は、国や地域によってさまざまです。ですから、日本人が素晴らしいと思っている価値観でも、海外ではそれが不可解であったり、時には全く違う観点からマイナスに評価されてしまうことがあるかもしれません。例えば、日本人が謙遜して遠慮すると、アメリカ人はその人を控えめで社会性のある人と思うのではなく、自信がなくフレンドリーではない人だと評価してしまうこともあるのです。だからこそ、自分の文化について英語で語る力が必要になります。

　つまり、価値観は決して善悪の基準ではなく、あくまでも相対的なものなのです。しかし、それが相手側の善悪の基準により、時と場合によって誤解され判断されるリスクがあるわけです。ですから、我々も自らの価値観をただ相手に押し付けることは危険だと思わなければなりません。

　自らの文化の土台となる価値観は、その国のアイデンティティでもあり、時にはプライドの源泉でもあるはずです。ということは同じように日本とは異なる価値観がその国や地域に住む人が大切に培っている常識となっていることも多々あるわけです。ですから、本書で語る日本の価値観や日本人の心の原点は、決してお国自慢ではないのだということを意識してほしいのです。

　一方で、そんな日本人ならではの価値観に従って、どう世界で活躍し、貢献できるかということを考えれば、それはそれで素晴らしいことといえましょう。なぜならば異なる価値観が混ざることで、よりお互いの理解が増え、そこから一つの文化背景だけでは創造できないシナジーが醸し出されるからです。

　この本で紹介する日本人の心を形成する価値観の中には、ともすれば日本人にとっても忘れ去られがちなものもあるかもしれません。しかし、これらの価値観が日本人の行動やコミュニケーションスタイルの土台となり、気付かれない

Preface

This book addresses the question of how to explain traditional Japanese values and ideas, across fourteen different themes, in English.

Culture varies widely between different countries and regions. Values prized by the Japanese can be incomprehensible to those in other countries, or even evaluated negatively based on radically different perspectives. For example, the self-effacing reserve common in Japan might be taken by an American as a sign of insecurity or unfriendliness rather than the mark of a modest, well-socialized individual. This is precisely why it is so vital to be able to discuss one's culture in English.

Values, in short, are not a matter of right and wrong; they are always relative. Nevertheless, they are at risk of being misunderstood in certain times and places based on an interlocutor's sense of right and wrong. We must, therefore, recognize the danger of unthinkingly imposing our values on others.

The values on which a culture is based become part of national identity and, at times, a source of pride. Values quite unlike Japan's are carefully cultivated common sense to those from the countries and regions where they are prevalent. For this reason, the values covered in this book, the wellspring of the Japanese heart and soul, should never be treated as patriotic boasts to be trumpeted about.

However, to consider how one might act and contribute on the global stage in accordance with uniquely Japanese values is, I think, a wonderful thing. This is because the meeting of different values deepens mutual understanding and cultivates a synergy that could not arise from any single cultural background.

Some of the values described in this book as formative elements in the Japanese heart and soul may have a tendency to be forgotten today even in Japan. However, Japanese behavior and communication styles are founded

ままにも受け継がれてきていることは確かです。ということは、本書を通して自らのルーツを見つめ直すこともできるかもしれません。その上で、もし何か海外の人との間でコミュニケーションが難しいと思ったとき、そうしたルーツがいかに自分の行動に影響を与えているかを探れば、相手との溝を埋める手段にもなるはずです。

　そしてまた、価値観は時と共に変化もします。今回はそのことを踏まえ、現在を生きる我々の価値観についても触れてみました。その上で現在の価値観にも微妙に何世紀にもわたって受け継がれた伝統的な思いの残り香があることにぜひ気づいてほしいのです。

　日本はともすれば世界の中でも最も「ミステリアス」な国だと言われてきました。その原因は欧米の人からみると真逆な行動が日本人にとっては当然の常識となっているからに他なりません。そんな一面を、本書を通して理解するのも面白いはずです。

　人は自分のことを論理的に語ることができにくいものです。あまりにも当たり前のことは、説明しにくいものです。英語であればなおさらです。本書がそんな困難を克服する一助となれば幸いです。

山久瀬洋二

on these values; they are still handed down, even if they go unnoticed. As a result, this book could be an opportunity for Japanese readers to rediscover their own roots. Reflecting on how those roots influence one's own behavior can offer guidance on how to bridge any gaps experienced when communicating with those from other countries.

Values also change with the times. In recognition of this fact, this book also touches on the values we live today. I encourage readers to note the ways in which even contemporary values bear subtle but indelible traces of traditional ideas handed down over the centuries.

Japan has often been called the world's most mysterious country. The reason for this is that certain kinds of behavior that are considered entirely normal in Japan seem topsy-turvy from a European or American perspective. I hope that readers of this book will enjoy coming to understand this aspect of culture as well.

It is not easy to talk about ourselves logically. The more obvious something seems, the harder it is to explain—particularly in a foreign language. I would be delighted if this book proved helpful to readers seeking to overcome these challenges.

Yamakuse Yoji

目次
Contents

1

和
わ
Harmony

和

「和」とは、そのまま訳せばharmonyです。

「和」はまた日本を表す別の表現でもあります。たとえば日本食のことを、日本人は和食ともいいます。日本の伝統的な服は和服と呼びます。

「和」とは、人と人とがいかに心地よく、共に過ごし、働くかということを表す価値観です。

日本は伝統的に、限られた土地を皆で耕作して、生活をしてきた農耕社会によって成り立ってきました。この社会を成り立たせるためには、村人が自らのニーズよりも、村全体のニーズを考え、他の人々と行動を共にして稲を植え、収穫をしなければなりません。

したがって、日本には、個人の力量や行動を価値基準の中心におく狩猟社会や移民社会とは異なる、常に相手との絆を気遣い、グループで行動することをよしとする価値基準が育まれました。それが「和」という価値観なのです。

日本人にとって「和」は、日本人の心の中に培われた全ての価値観の要となる考え方なのです。

和

Harmony

While the Chinese character for *wa* directly means "harmony," it is also used to mean "Japan." For example, Japanese cuisine is known as *wa-shoku* and Japanese clothing is known as *wa-fuku*.

"Harmony" is a basic value defined as the ability of people to cooperate pleasantly and work together well.

Japan is a country whose traditions developed out of an agricultural society where people were forced to work closely together on a limited amount of land. In order to maintain this type of society, the needs of the village were more important than the needs of the individual, as all labored together to plant the rice and harvest the crop.

Therefore, as opposed to hunter- or immigrant-based societies, where a high value is placed on the power or actions of the individual, a society developed in Japan where the value is placed on understanding those with whom one must interact and on taking action in groups. That is the definition of *wa*.

Wa is at the heart of what has been necessary to nurture everything in the Japanese value system.

- □ そのまま directly
- □ 伝統的な traditional
- □ 心地よく pleasantly
- □ 価値観 value
- □ 土地を耕作する cultivate the land
- □ 農耕社会 agricultural society
- □ 成り立つ develop, maintain
- □ 稲を植える plant rice
- □ 収穫する harvest a crop
- □ したがって therefore
- □ 力量 power
- □ 狩猟社会や移民社会 hunter- or immigrant-based societies
- □ 相手との絆 bond with one's partner
- □ 気遣う concern for
- □ 〜をよしとする approve of -ing
- □ 培われた nurtured
- □ 要 heart

謙譲 と 謙遜

「和」をもって人とつき合うとき、お互いが自我を出しあって、自らの能力を強調し合ってばかりいると、物事がうまく進みません。日本人はこういうとき、むしろ自らの能力を抑え、相手に敬意を払いながら、相手との関係を構築します。この自分をへりくだり、相手に対して敢えて自らの能力を表明しない考え方を「謙譲」といいます。

相手も、「私は何もわかりませんが」といわれると、それを言葉通りには受け止めません。逆に日本では、能力のある人ほど、自分のことを低く表現することがよいこととされているために、このようにいう相手は、かえって尊敬されるのです。

この「謙譲」の価値観を実際の言葉遣いで表すとき、人は「謙遜する」という表現を使います。この言葉こそは、日本人の極めて大切な行動原理となっているのです。

「謙遜する」という行為は、時には家族や会社の同僚を紹介するときに使われます。自分の子供を紹介するとき、「何もできない愚息ですが」などといって紹介する習わしがそれにあたります。

自らの能力を率直に表現することをよしとする文化背景からきた外国の人には、この日本人の行動原理がわからず、戸惑いを覚えることがよくあるようです。

「実るほど頭を垂れる稲穂かな」という日本人の好きな言葉があります。また、「能ある鷹は爪を隠す」という言葉も有名です。これは全て「謙遜」することの美学を伝える言葉なのです。

Modesty

When using *wa* as the basis for a relationship, things will not go smoothly if both parties egotistically emphasize their own capabilities. A Japanese person would in fact downplay his own capabilities while paying respect to the other person and build the relationship in that way. This concept of putting oneself below another and not presuming to show one's capabilities is called *kenjō*.

One cannot take the words at their face value when one is told: "I don't know anything." In Japan, the greater the capabilities of a person, the more modestly he will state those capabilities, and thus in fact such persons are more respected.

When stating the value of *kenjō* in a sentence, it is common to use the word *kenson*, as in *kenson suru* ("being modest"). *Kenson* is a very important word in Japanese, reflecting the basic principles of the culture.

The concept of *kenson* is often used when introducing a member of one's family or company. This is evident in the phrase "good-for-nothing son" when introducing one's son, for example.

It seems that much confusion is created by the Japanese using this principle of *kenson* with non-Japanese whose cultures value straight forward expression of one's capabilities.

"The heavier the stock of rice, the more its head is lowered" is an expression well liked by the Japanese. "A wise hawk hides its talons" is another well-known phrase. These all convey the beauty of the concept of *kenson*.

□和をもって using *wa* as the basis
□自我を出す show oneself
□敬意を払う pay respect
□関係を構築する build the relationship
□へりくだる put oneself below another
□敢えて〜する dare to
□かえって (but) in fact
□実際の言葉遣い actual wording
□行動原理 behavioral principle
□同僚 coworker
□愚息 good-for-nothing son
□あたる correspond
□率直に表現する straight forward expression
□戸惑いを覚える get bewildered
□頭を垂れる lower one's head
□稲穂 stock of rice
□能ある wise

遠慮

「和」を保つために最も考えなければならないことは、相手のことを 慮 る気持ちです。相手の状況を考えて、自らの行動を**抑制し**、相手に迷惑にならないようにすることを「遠慮」といいます。

遠慮の「遠」は遠くを、そして「慮」は**思いめぐらす**ことを意味します。**つまり、**つねに先に思いを巡らして、相手に対応する**心がけ**が「遠慮」なのです。躊躇という言葉がありますが、これは何かをすれば状況が悪くなるのではと恐れて行動を抑制することを意味します。

それに対して「遠慮」は、むしろそうなる前にしっかりと相手のことを考えて、相手のために**行動を差し控える**未来に向けた**心構え**なのです。

相手に聞くまでもなく、自らが相手の気持ちを判断して、たとえば「今この話をすると相手が不快だろうから、遠慮して別の機会にしておこう」などと考えるのです。

言葉をもって明快に自らのニーズを伝え、それに対応することをよしとする欧米の文化からしてみると、この「遠慮」という考え方を理解することは困難です。躊躇がさらに未来の行動へと延長すると思えばわかりやすいのかもしれませんが、国際舞台では、日本人は**ついつい**「遠慮」をしすぎて、自らの意思を伝えるチャンスを失っているようでもありますね。

現在では、「遠慮」という言葉をそのまま、「禁止する」と同じ意味に使うことも**多々あります**。「タバコはご遠慮ください」といえば、禁煙を丁寧に相手に伝えることになるのです。

Reserve

To maintain *wa*, it is always very important to give careful consideration to the feelings of the person with whom one is dealing. Understanding the circumstances of the other person and controlling one's actions so as not to cause trouble to that person is called *enryo*.

The first Chinese character of *en* in *enryo* means "distant," while the second character of *ryo* means "to think about." In other words, always thinking ahead about how to deal with other people is *enryo*. The word *chūcho* means "to hesitate," and is used in describing a situation in which a person refrains from taking action due to fear that circumstances will worsen.

Enryo, on the other hand, means thinking ahead before a situation develops, taking fully into account the other person, and then refraining from action based on those circumstances.

Without asking, one should be able to judge the feelings of the other person and decide if *enryo* is necessary. For example, "If I bring this up now, I'll make the other person feel uncomfortable, so I'll wait until another time."

In a culture where people are expected to speak up and make their needs known, with action being taken based on those requests, it is difficult for Westerners to understand the concept of *enryo*. Westerners, they may be able to understand *enryo* as an extension of *chūcho*, or hesitation, but too often the Japanese lose the chance to speak out on issues on the international stage due to their tendency towards *enryo*.

Nowadays the word *enryo* is also often used to mean "prohibited." For example, *tabako wa go-enryo kudasai* is a polite way of telling people that smoking is prohibited.

□ 慮る give careful consideration
□ 抑制する control one's action
□ ～にならないようにする so as not to cause
□ 思いめぐらす think about
□ つまり in other words
□ 心がけ care
□ 躊躇する hesitate
□ それに対して on the other hand
□ 行動を差し控える refrain from action
□ 心構え preparedness
□ ～からしてみると from a ~ point of view
□ ついつい too often
□ 多々ある many

場
ば

「遠慮」という考え方を理解するために必要なのがこの「場」という概念です。「場」とはいうまでもなく場所を意味します。そして、どういう場所でどのような行動をするかということを暗に示したのが「場」という概念なのです。

この「場」という考え方は、欧米でもあるようです。たとえば、結婚式を例にとれば、正式に教会や神社で行う儀式と、その後で披露宴などのパーティーでの人々の行動は自ずと違ってきます。儀式の間はしきたりに従い、パーティーでは比較的自由に人々は交流します。すなわち、「場」が違えば、それぞれ「場」に合った行動が求められるのです。

日本では日本人の価値観や行動様式に従って、外国人には見えない「場」がたくさんあります。お客さんとの正式な打合せの「場」での態度や、上司の前という「場」でのものの言い方、またはくだけたお酒の席という「場」での発言など、「場」によって人の行動が細かく変わり、時にはその「場」の状況によって、人は行動を差し控え「遠慮」することもあるのです。

「場をわきまえる」という言葉がありますが、「場」の状況をしっかりと理解して、その時に何をすべきかを的確に判断することが、日本での礼儀作法の第一歩といえます。

微妙な「場」の違いに気付かない外国人は、時には不作法をしてしまうかもしれません。

Place, Situation

To understand the thinking behind *enryo*, the concept of *ba* is necessary. It goes without saying that *ba* refers to "place." What actions happen in what place is implicit within the concept of *ba*.

The idea of *ba*, "place," also exists in the West. For example, in the case of a wedding, the actions of people at the ceremony at the church or temple are naturally different from people's actions at the reception afterwards. At the ceremony there are strict practices to follow, while at the reception people interact in a relatively free manner. In other words, because the *ba*, "place," is different, different actions are required.

There are many *ba* in Japan where the basic values and actions of the Japanese are employed, and these *ba* may be difficult for the non-Japanese to understand. The words and actions of a formal meeting with a customer will differ from those in a meeting with one's boss, and will differ again in the informal atmosphere of a night out on the town. At times, the concept of *enryo* will be necessary within the context of a particular *ba*.

The expression *ba wo wakimaeru* means to clearly understand the circumstances of a particular *ba*. Being able to make proper judgments about what to do based on the particular time and place is a first step towards truly grasping the basics of Japanese etiquette.

Sometimes a non-Japanese, not understanding the subtleties of a particular *ba*, will commit a faux pas.

□ 概念 concept
□ 〜はいうまでもない It goes without saying that
□ 暗に示す implicit
□ 例にとれば in the case of
□ 儀式 ceremony
□ 自ずと naturally
□ しきたり a strict practice to follow
□ 交流する interact
□ すなわち in other words
□ くだけた informal
□ 差し控える withhold
□ 場をわきまえる clearly understand the circumstances
□ 何をすべきか about what to do
□ 礼儀作法 etiquette
□ 時には sometimes

根回し
<small>ね　まわ</small>

　人との「和」を保ち、賢く自らの意見を 公 で発表するために、日本人は適切な「場」を選び、「間」も考慮して慎重に人とその情報を共有してゆきます。こうした日本人の行動様式の典型が「根回し」という意思伝達方法なのです。

　会議の「場」でいきなりプレゼンテーションを行うと、場合によっては上司や関係者と意見の対立を生むリスクがあります。それを避けるために、関係する人に会議の前にその情報を伝えたり、必要に応じて提案内容を調整することを「根回し」というのです。

　「根回し」が首尾よく行われていれば、会議の「場」で紛糾することなく、案件が承認されるわけです。

　非公式で「根回し」をするのはよくあることです。時には夕食やゴルフなどの会合といった職場から離れたプライベートな「場」で行われることもあります。

　そして、「根回し」をしっかりと繰り返すことで、人と公然と対立せずに、情報が共有され、企画やアイデアに関する情報が共有されるのです。

　根回しのそもそもの意味は、木を移植するときに、根を掘り起こし、それを傷つかないように丸く包んで移動させる方法のことです。

　すなわち、木を移植するときと同じように、関係者一人一人と話すことによって、人の輪をつくり、それを包み込んで公式の場に持ち込む方法が「根回し」なのです。

　「根回し」は今でも日本の組織のあちこちで実践されています。外国の人が「根回し」の外におかれないためには、日本人と、より気軽に接触し、時には夜、一緒にお酒を飲むなどして、日本人の輪の中に入ってゆくことが肝要です。

　これは、日本では公式な場だけではなく、個々人のレベルでの密なコミュニケーションがいかに大切かを物語る、象徴的な概念であるともいえそうです。

Lobbying

In order to preserve harmony (*wa*) when going "on the record" with an opinion, the Japanese will cautiously share information with others after careful consideration of the place and the timing. A very typical Japanese form of communicating one's will in this situation would be *nemawashi* (literally "loosening the roots").

If one presents a proposal for the first time right at a meeting, there is a risk that one's superiors or others affected by the proposal will have a different opinion. Avoiding this risk by consulting prior to the meeting with key persons and adjusting one's proposal as necessary is called *nemawashi* ("lobbying").

If one has done a thorough job of *nemawashi*, there should be little opposition at the meeting and the proposal should be approved.

It is common for *nemawashi* to take place outside the office, perhaps over dinner or while playing golf or at some other private setting (*ba*).

Through the repetition of *nemawashi*, there will naturally be fewer conflicts, with better sharing of plans and ideas.

The original meaning of *nemawashi* is to "loosen the roots," or in other words, to carefully dig a circle around the roots in order to preserve them when moving a plant or tree.

Similarly, when conducting *nemawashi* for a proposal, one is trying to carefully create a circle of consensus among the key people involved to move the proposal unscathed to the formal setting of a meeting.

Even now the use of *nemawashi* is quite common in organizations in Japan. It is important for non-Japanese to also move into "the circle of consensus" when conducting business in Japan by spending more time in *nemawashi* over drinks or in other informal settings.

This says just how important informal, one-on-one settings are in communicating in Japan. *Nemawashi* is indeed a representative concept of Japanese values.

□ 公で public
□ 考慮する consider
□ 典型 typical pattern
□ 意思伝達方法 method of communication
□ 会議の前に prior to the meeting
□ 調整する adjust
□ 首尾よく行う do a thorough job
□ 紛糾する become complicated
□ 案件 proposal
□ ～するのはよくあること It is common to
□ ～といった or some such
□ そもそもの意味 original meaning
□ 移植する transplant
□ 人の輪をつくる build a network of people
□ あちこちで実践されている practiced here and there
□ 外におかれる be left out of the party
□ 肝要な essential
□ 密な close
□ いかに how
□ 象徴的な representative

2

型
かた

Form,
Way of Doing Things

型
かた

　「和」という価値観で、農耕社会を基軸とする日本社会でのコミュニケーションの方法について説明しました。そして、自分の考えや能力を強く主張することなく社会を運営してゆくために、日本人が発展させてきた価値観が、ここに紹介する「型」という考え方です。

　古代から、農業での豊作を神に感謝し、人と人との絆を強くするために、人々は様々な儀式をつくってゆきました。その後、身分や階級制度が社会に浸透する中で、さらに人と人との上下関係を具体的に表すための作法やマナーが生み出されます。

　儀式や作法は、全ての人がその様式に従うために、それぞれの「場」での行動様式、すなわち「型」が生み出され、それによって社会の多くの場面で、様々な「型」が尊重されるようになったのです。

　今では、「型」は日本人の生活様式、行動のいたるところにみることができます。ビジネスでの名刺交換、相撲での取組前の儀式、そしてごく日常でいうならば、お酒の席での杯の受け方やつぎ方などが例です。

　また、武道や伝統の専門領域のことを習得するためには、まずそこで培われた「型」を学ぶことが要求されます。「型」をマスターしてこそ、人々は次のステップに進むことができるのです。「型」を習得するという価値観は、日本人が物事を進めるにあたって、どのように対処すべきかという方程式をまず理解しようとするのが重要です。まず、行動し、試行錯誤をしながら進めるのではなく、「いかに（how）」の答えを見つけてから進もうとする考え方を日本人は好むのです。

　「型」は、日本人の行動様式、ビジネスの進め方を理解する上でも大切な価値観なのです。

Form

We have already discussed how *wa* ("harmony") was an essential social value in the communication style of feudal Japan. Here we will introduce *kata* ("form"), another Japanese value that promotes social cooperation over one's individual thoughts or capabilities.

In ancient times, people in agricultural communities gave thanks to the gods, creating various ceremonies that helped to strengthen bonds with other people. Later, as a class system developed, additional forms of etiquette came into being as a means of expressing the difference in rank among people.

To ensure that all people would appropriately follow the various ceremonies and etiquette, the concept of *kata* developed, whereby a particular *kata* ("form") would be followed at a particular place and time.

Nowadays, one can see *kata* in action in all aspects of Japanese life. The exchange of name cards, the pre-bout rituals of sumo, even the relatively mundane act of pouring and receiving a cup of sake—these are all examples.

In *budō* ("martial arts") or in other traditional disciplines, one must first cultivate *kata*. The more quickly one is able to master *kata*, the quicker one will advance to the next step. For the Japanese, before tackling a project, it is essential that they first understand the process by which that project will be completed. It is not proper to take random actions, trying to accomplish things through trial and error; rather one must first understand the answer to the question: How?

Kata is an important concept in understanding how the Japanese operate in business and in other fields.

☐ 基軸とする be based on
☐ 豊作 rich harvest
☐ 階級制度 class system
☐ 社会に浸透する permeate society
☐ 生み出される come into being
☐ 様式に従う follow a pattern
☐ それによって whereby
☐ いたるところに in all aspects
☐ ごく日常の relatively mundane
☐ 次のステップに進む advance to the next step
☐ 〜するのは重要だ It is essential that
☐ 試行錯誤 trial and error
☐ 理解する上で in understanding

修練
しゅうれん

「型」を学ぶときは、何度も同じことを繰り返しながら、柔道での体の動きや習字での筆の使い方、あるいは踊るときの振る舞い方などを習得します。もちろん、「型」にはそれぞれ合理的な理由があったはずです。しかし、それがいかに合理的であるかを理解するためには、ただ黙々と「型」によって表現されるパターンを覚えてゆく必要があります。

教える者は、得てして理由を伝えることなく、教える者が納得するまで、学習者に「型」を教え込みます。日本には伝統的にフィードバックという文化がなく、学ぶ者は教える者を信じ、その指示に問いかけることなく従ってゆきました。

「型」の習得には時には何年もの修業期間が必要です。そしてしっかりと「型」を学んだ後に、はじめて学習者はその合理性に気付き、そこからさらに技量を発展させてゆくのです。

この「型」を学ぶ厳しい過程を「修練」といいます。そして、「修練」というものの考え方は、ビジネスのノウハウを習得してゆく上での、上司と部下の関係にもみてとることができるのです。フィードバックがなく、ただ厳しく指導する上司は、最近でこそ少なくなりました。とはいえ、今なお、欧米人が日本人を上司にもったとき、フィードバックの少なさに戸惑うことがよくあります。

確かに、このフィードバックの少ない日本流の指導方法は、欧米のマネージメントとは根本的に異なっているようです。

Discipline

When learning a new *kata* ("form"), one will repeat the same action numerous times, whether it is a jūdō throw or the strokes of a calligraphy brush or the steps of a dance. Of course there is ultimately a logic to all *kata*, but in order to truly understand that logic, it is necessary for the student to continue to silently repeat the action.

The teacher does not tell the student why something must be done in a certain way; he simply continues to have the student repeat the action until he, the teacher, is satisfied. In Japan traditionally there is no culture of "feedback." The student trusts the teacher and follows the directions of the teacher without questioning.

In certain cases, it may be necessary to spend many years in training to master *kata*. Only then, after the *kata* has been mastered, does the student really first understand the true logic of his movements, and then from there he may further develop his skill.

This demanding process of learning a *kata* is called *shūren*. *Shūren* may be seen in the business world in the relationship between subordinate and boss, although in recent years the example of the boss who manages his subordinates harshly without any feedback has become rarer. That said, Westerners who have Japanese bosses are still often puzzled by the lack of feedback.

It is true that this lack of feedback is different from the communication and management style in the West.

□ あるいは or
□ 振る舞い方 steps, how to behave
□ 合理的な理由 reasonable reasons
□ 黙々と silently
□ 得てして tend to
□ 〜が納得するまで until someone is satisfied
□ 問いかける question
□ 技量 skill
□ 過程 process
□ みてとる see
□ 最近でこそ although in recent years
□ 戸惑う be puzzled
□ 根本的に fundamentally

匠
たくみ

　最近、日本では伝統的な「技」をもって工芸や手仕事に携わる人が見直されてきています。こうした人々のことを「匠」と呼びます。

　「匠」は、長い年月をかけて「型」を習得し、そこからさらに「技」を磨いて、技能を極めた職人のことを意味しています。

　細かい手仕事など、人間にしかできない技術をもって伝統的な作品を作る職人は、機械化と合理化の中で次第に廃れてゆきました。しかし、最近の日本の伝統的な職人芸を見直そうという動きの中で、各所で「匠」の「技」が再発見されてきています。

　実は、自動車業界などの製造業においても、研磨など、人の勘や微細な技量を必要とする分野で、「技」をいかに次世代に伝えてゆくか試行錯誤の努力がなされています。

　「匠」の「技」をいかに若い世代に伝えるかというとき、果たして伝統的な師匠と弟子との関係を今の若い世代が受け入れてゆけるのかという課題があるのです。師匠を常に尊敬し、文字通り人生を預けるようにして技術を磨くのか、それとも「スキル」として実用的な技術の習得に努めるのか。難しい選択といえましょう。

　特に、日本の伝統的な会社が、国際環境で海外の人を育成するとき、日本流の師弟関係は通用しません。時代に合った、「匠」の「技」の伝承が求められているのです。

Craft

Recently those involved in traditional handicrafts in Japan have come to be viewed in a new light. In Japanese, these people are said to have a *takumi* ("craft").

These craftsmen develop their *takumi* through many years of mastering a *kata* ("form"), followed by further polishing of their *waza* ("skill"). Such craftsmen, who create traditional items that can only be made by hand, have been dwindling in numbers in this age of continued industrialization and rationalization. However, as the products created by these craftsmen have been reevaluated in recent years, so also have the *takumi* these artisans possess.

In fact, in the automobile and other industries, efforts are being made through trial and error to pass on to the next generation grinding and other skills that require detailed handiwork and intuition.

In trying to pass on to the next generation various *takumi* and *waza*, there is the issue of whether or not younger people will accept the traditional teacher-student relationship. Will they respect their teacher, entrusting their lives to him as they polish their *waza*, or will they simply work to master a narrow skill? It is a difficult choice to make.

It is not possible to use this traditional teacher-student model when training people outside of Japan. In that case, a new model for *takumi* and *waza* must be used.

□ 工芸 craftwork
□ 携わる involved in
□ 見直される be reevaluated
□ 廃れる dwindle
□ 各所で in various places
□ 再発見される be rediscovered
□ 研磨 grinding
□ 勘 intuition
□ 微細な detailed
□ 〜を必要とする require
□ 次世代 next generation
□ 努力がなされている efforts are being made
□ 〜に伝える pass on to
□ 人生を預ける devote one's life
□ 通用しない it is not possible to use
□ 伝承 hand down (information)

3

道
みち
Way

道
_{みち}

　「型」が技術を学ぶための具体的なノウハウであるとすれば、「道」は「型」を学び、その技量を高めてゆくための精神的な価値観を示す言葉です。

　「道」は「みち」と発音される場合と、中国語のdaoからの「どう」と発音される場合があります。「道」は英語のroadあるいはwayにあたり、人が歩き、車が通るところを指す言葉です。その「道」を人生になぞらえることは、欧米でもよくあることです。そして、日本では、「型」の学習を「道」になぞらえて考えます。「道」は人がしなければならないことを示す言葉として、人生の色々な場面での処し方、道徳律を示す言葉としても使用されているのです。

　日本人は伝統的に「道」というコンセプトを好み、人としての生き方を語るときにこの言葉を使用します。たとえば、「人としての道をはずす」といえば、不道徳な生き方をしていることを示します。また、「道を極める」といえば、匠の境地に至り、その分野の極意を極めた達人となることを意味します。

　したがって、日本人は、学習し、技を磨かなければならない事柄に「道」という言葉を頻繁に付加します。

　華道といえば、生け花を習得するプロセスを指し、剣道はもっと直裁に日本流のフェンシングとしてスポーツの名前になっています。柔道も同様ですし、日本古来の宗教も神道といわれ、この場合は「しんとう」と発音されます。

　「道」の考え方は、遠くに至るまで続く学習方法を示すことによって、そのhowに従って生きようとする日本人の文化背景に深く根ざした価値観であるといえましょう。

Way, Road

If *kata* is the concrete know-how by which a skill is learned, then *michi* is the spiritual value by which that skill is further strengthened.

The Chinese character for *michi* can also be read as *dō* (from the Chinese "dao"). In English, *michi* would be translated as "way" or "road," the path used by a person to walk or by a vehicle to travel. The same as in Japanese for *michi*, the words "way" or "road" are often used in Western languages as metaphors for life. In Japan, *michi* is also often used as a metaphor for the process of learning various *kata* as one proceeds down the road of life, doing what one must to become a more virtuous person.

The Japanese have traditionally liked the concept of *michi* and will often use it when describing the type of life lead by a person. For example, if a person is leading an immoral life, they will say that that person is *fudōtoku* ("not on the road of virtue"). As another example, when a person pushes his skill to the utmost and is on the cutting edge of a field, the Japanese say that he is "taking the road to its ultimate destination" (*michi wo kiwameru*).

The word *michi* is therefore often used when the Japanese are describing circumstances where they must learn or polish a skill.

Kadō (written with the characters for "flower" and "way") is the art of flower arrangement; *kendō* ("sword" and "way") is the martial art of fencing; *jūdō* ("flexible" and "way") is another martial art; and *Shintō* ("gods" and "way"—here pronounced *tō*) is the native religion of Japan.

The concept of *michi* reflects the approach taken to learning since ancient times in Japan; it is a social value with deep roots in Japanese culture.

□ 具体的な concrete
□ ～にあたる be equivalent to
□ なぞらえる use something as a metaphor
□ ～の処し方 way of dealing with
□ 道徳律 moral law
□ 人として as a person
□ 道をはずす lead an immoral life
□ 不道徳な immoral
□ 道を極める taking the road to its ultimate destination
□ 境地に至る push one's skill to the utmost
□ その分野の極意を極めた on the cutting edge of a field
□ 頻繁に often
□ 付加する append
□ 直截に directly
□ 至る get to
□ ～に深く根ざした with deep roots in

37

道理
どう り

「道理」とは、ロジックを意味した言葉です。

「道理」の「理」という言葉は、「ことわり」ともよみ、それは物事の本来あるべき姿を示す言葉です。また、ロジックにかなった当然の帰結をも意味する言葉です。その言葉に「道」の概念が加わり「道理」となるわけで、それは、人が道徳律に従った行動をし、ロジックもしっかりとしていることを指し示すときに使用されるのです。

封建時代からずっと日本人が培ってきた価値観にそって、たとえば年上の人を敬い、師匠や上司に敬意を払って、それにふさわしい行動をすることは、日本では「道理に叶った」行動であるといわれます。

すなわち、単に理屈が通り、ロジックに支えられているのではなく、そこにしっかりとした道徳的なバックアップがあることが「道理」の意味するところなのです。そして、その道徳は、日本の伝統的な価値観に支えられているわけで、必ずしも万国全てに受け入れられるものではありません。

人生のあり方を示す「道」という価値観が、日本人のロジックの構成に大きく影響を与えている証拠が、この「道理」という言葉なのです。

Reason

The English translation for *dōri* would be "reason."

The Chinese character of *ri* in *dōri* is also read as *kotowari* and means the "proper structure" of things, or in other words, "reason" or "truth." By adding the character for *dō* ("way") to *ri*, we come up with *dōri*, or the proper "structure" of a person, with the concept of "reason" also clearly expressed.

In keeping with social values which have been cultivated since feudal times, the Japanese use the phrase *dōri ni kanatta* ("following reason") to describe the actions of a person who pays proper respect to his elders, teachers, or superiors.

In other words, it is not enough to simply put forth clever arguments; *dōri* requires that one must also have a moral backbone supporting one's words. As this morality is based on traditional values nurtured in Japan, it is not something that one can expect to be accepted in all countries around the world.

Proof that the social value of *michi*, or *dō*, is imbedded in the concept of reason can be seen in the very word *dōri*, which includes the character for *dō*.

□ 理 reason, truth

□ あるべき姿 proper structure

□ 当然の帰結 a natural conclusion

□ 指し示す indicate

□ 封建時代 feudal period

□ 培ってきた have been cultivated

□ ふさわしい appropriate

□ 道理に叶った following reason

□ 単に理屈が通る just makes sense

□ 意味するところ meaning

□ 〜に支えられている be based on

□ 万国全て all countries round the world

武士道

11

「道」という概念を最も端的に表しているのが、封建時代に武士が自らのあるべき生き方として心に刻んでいた「武士道」という価値観です。

「武士道」については、明治時代の思想家であり外交官でもある新渡戸稲造が『武士道』という名著を残しています。

新渡戸稲造は、ちょうど欧米でのキリスト教のように、それを日本人の道徳律の源泉であるとして、封建時代から培ってきた日本人の価値観、善悪を判断する基準としての道徳律が「武士道」であると説いているのです。

武士のことを別のいい方で侍と呼び、そちらの方が欧米では有名になってしまいました。武士とは刀をもって戦い、時には主君や村や町を敵から守る人のことを指します。侍は、その武士が封建制度の枠組みにそって主君に仕えてゆく中で生まれた言葉です。

ちょうど西欧の騎士のように、主君に対して忠誠を誓い、必要とあれば命も捧げて主君とその領土を守り抜くことが侍の勤めでした。そのために常に精神的、肉体的な鍛錬を怠らず、死をも克服できる強い人格形成に努めることが、侍のあるべき姿とされたのです。こうした侍の人生観と、それに育まれた行動様式が武士の「道」、すなわち「武士道」なのです。

忠誠を貫くために常に何を学び、いかに振る舞うべきか。人の上に立つ身分である侍が常に心がけなければならない義務や掟はどのようなものか。「武士道」は、個人の欲望を抑え、質素な中で清廉に生き、死を畏れずに主君を守り抜くことの大切さを教えていました。そして、侍は、寡黙で、物事に動じる事なく、常に平常心で危急に対処する精神力が求められたのです。

The Way of the Warrior

The concept of *michi,* or *dō,* was expressed in its purest form by *bushi* ("warriors") during the feudal period in the way of life known as *bushidō.*

The Meiji Era (1868–1912) philosopher and diplomat Nitobe Inazo wrote a well-known book entitled *Bushidō: The Soul of Japan.*

In this book, Nitobe made the argument that *bushidō* is to Japan as Christianity is to the West, in the sense that *bushidō* is the source of moral law in Japan, providing the basis for judging right and wrong.

Another expression for *bushi* is *samurai,* a word that has become better known in the West. The *bushi* fought with swords, and at times could be called on to protect their masters or villages or towns from enemies. The *samurai* were *bushi* who, in the feudal structure of the time, served their lords.

As with the knights of the West, the *samurai* swore allegiance to their lords and were prepared to sacrifice their lives in defense of him and his land. To fulfill their role, the *samurai* trained hard both physically and mentally to develop a fortitude that could withstand the constant threat of death. This way of viewing life and the actions which grew out of such a view were the *dō* ("way") which the *bushi* traversed; hence the word *bushidō.*

In the pursuit of loyalty, the *bushi* were always concerned about what to learn and how to act. As persons of higher rank than others, what type of responsibilities and rules did the *samurai* in fact have to keep in mind? *Bushidō* taught the importance of controlling individual desires, not fearing death, and leading a simple life of integrity as one protected one's lord. *Samurai* were also expected to be taciturn, unswayed by events around them, able to remain calm and respond to danger at any time.

□ 端的に in a nutshell
□ 思想家 thinker
□ 外交官 diplomat
□ 名著 great book
□ 源泉 source
□ ～であると説く make the argument that
□ 主君 master
□ 封建制度の枠組みにそって in the feudal structure of time
□ 仕える serve
□ 忠誠を誓う swear allegiance to
□ 命を捧げる sacrifice one's life
□ 鍛練を怠らず be diligent in one's training
□ 克服する overcome
□ 強い人格形成に努める develop a fortitude
□ 人生観 way of viewing life
□ ～を貫く in the pursuit of
□ 質素な simple
□ 清廉に with integrity
□ 寡黙 taciturn
□ 動じる be shaken
□ 危急 danger

現在でも日本には、個人の利益よりも会社の責務を優先し、だまって命ぜられた業務をこなすビジネスの環境が見受けられます。特に上に立つ者は、部下の過ちも自らの責任として引き受けようとすることを美徳とする風習が残っています。

　若い世代にこの「武士道」が廃れてきたと嘆く年配の人も多くいます。そして、もちろん、昔でも現実が「武士道」の理想と乖離したことも多々ありました。

　しかし、これからも日本人の価値観の一番奥底に、「武士道」的な発想が、時代によって変化しながらも、受け継がれていくのではないでしょうか。

In today's business world in Japan this way of thinking can still be found, as duty to one's company comes before individual profit, and company employees take care of requested assignments with few questions. It can also be seen in the case of managers who take responsibility for the mistakes of their subordinates.

Many older Japanese are disappointed that the younger generation has fallen away from the principles of *bushidō*. Of course, even in the past, the reality of *bushidō* was not always aligned with the ideal.

However, even as the times continue to change, it seems likely that *bushidō* will remain at the heart of Japanese social values.

□責務 responsibility
□〜をこなす handle
□見受けられる be seen
□美徳とする regard as a virtue
□〜と乖離する not aligned with
□奥底 at the bottom
□〜ながらも even as

12

業
<ruby>ぎょう</ruby>

「業」とは、直訳すればトレーニングということになるのでしょうか。しかし、その意味するところは、「克己心」を培うために日常的に厳しい義務を己に課してゆくことなのです。

それは、ちょうど僧侶が悟りを目指して行う修行に通じるものがあります。実際日本では、山奥の厳しい環境で修行をすることを、「業」を行うと表現します。

「型」を学ぶときの「修練」も、ある意味では「業」であるといえましょう。以前、アメリカ人の著者、ロバート・ホワイティングが日本の野球を単なるスポーツとしてではなく、剣道や柔道と同じく、野球道であると評論しました。

それは、日本人が野球の練習をするときに、ただ技能を磨くのではなく、野球場という自らを鍛える場への敬意を学ぶために行う清掃から、先輩への礼儀作法、さらに一見野球の技術とは関係のない禅寺での座禅まで、精神的な側面を極めて重くみるトレーニングを重ねていることを彼がみたからです。まさに、野球を極めるための「業」をしているのだと、ロバート・ホワイティングは思ったのでしょう。

「業」という精神修業の方法は、現在のビジネスでの新人研修にも多く取り入れられています。

「業」は日本人のトレーニングに関する考え方の基本にある価値観で、何かを成し遂げるための長い「道」を進む上で大切な考え方なのです。

Training

If one must translate *gyō*, the closest word in English would probably be "training." However, this would be "training" in the sense of tasking oneself with the demanding responsibility of working hard day-to-day to cultivate one's *kokkishin* ("self-denial").

Buddhist priests do such training when they are seeking enlightenment (*satori*). In Japan, when one does such tough training deep in the mountains, one is said to be "conducting *gyō*" (*gyō wo okonau*).

The *shūren* ("discipline") used when one is learning *kata* ("forms") may be said to be a type of *gyō*. Robert Whiting, an American author, has written that Japanese baseball is in fact not a sport but rather a discipline, *yakyūdō*, along the same lines as *kendō* or *jūdō*.

He points out that Japanese players do not simply practice baseball; rather they also place emphasis on the spiritual side in their training—paying respect to the ball field by keeping it clean, being properly deferential to their seniors, and even going so far as to sit in meditation in *Zen* temples. It must have been very clear to Whiting that the players were employing a particularly Japanese form of training, *gyō*, in order to reach the top of their game.

In today's business world, many aspects of *gyō* are also used in the mental or spiritual training of workers.

For the Japanese, *gyō* is an essential value in all training; it is an important aspect of the *michi* ("road") one travels in seeking to accomplish anything.

- □ 克己心 spirit of self-denial
- □ 己に課す impose on oneself
- □ 悟り enlightenment
- □ 山奥 deep in the mountains
- □ 著者 author
- □ 評論する critique
- □ 技能 skill
- □ 先輩 senior
- □ 禅寺 Zen temple
- □ 座禅 seated Zen meditation
- □ 〜を重くみる place emphasis on
- □ 極める reach the top
- □ 精神修業 the mental or spiritual training
- □ 新人研修 newcomer training
- □ 取り入れられている be incorporated in
- □ 成し遂げる accomplish

求道
(ぐどう)

13

「業」を行い、自らが極めようとしている事柄に対して熱心に学習したり修行したりすることを「求道」と言います。

「道」を極めるために、しっかり修行し、自らを律する行為が「業」であるならば、そうした「業」を真摯に行う心がけが「求道」の精神です。

「道」という価値観を重んずる日本人は、「道」を極めるためにいかに努力し、目標に向けて「修練」を重ねるかということに強い関心を示します。「道」を極めるためのこうしたプロセスへの美学がそこに見受けられます。

仮に結果が思わしくなくても、そこに至るプロセスにおいて努力を重ねていれば、人はそれを評価し尊敬します。「求道」の精神こそが、結果以上に求められているのです。

ある意味で、結果重視の欧米型のビジネス文化からみるならば、「求道」の精神やプロセスを重んずる日本人の行動様式は非合理的にみえるかもしれません。

しかし、日本人からみるならば、結果を得ることそのものよりも、努力することで得られる経験や精神的な高みのほうがより重要なのです。

その経験が培った強い精神力があれば、たとえそこでの結果が思わしくないとしても、他の「場」において、しっかりと物事に取り組むことができるというわけです。

武士道においても、もしその人が精神鍛錬をしっかりと行えば、結果は自ずとついてくると教えられます。

試合に勝つことは、訓練を重ねてきたことの、一つの結果に過ぎないというわけです。

Seeking the Truth

When one trains and studies hard to thoroughly master something, this is called *gudō* ("seeking the truth").

If one defines *gyō* as the act of doing such training in order to find one's way (*michi*), then one can think of *gudō* as the sincere spirit employed in doing one's *gyō*.

For the Japanese, who highly value the concept of *michi*, there is a strong interest in how one disciplines oneself as one works hard to find one's way and reach a goal. One can see the aesthetic of seeking one's way in the process itself.

Even if the results are not what were hoped for, people will positively judge the effort made in the process. It is precisely in the spirit of *gudō* that something more than simply results is expected.

From the perspective of Westerners, who place a heavy emphasis on results in their business culture, the spirit of *gudō*, with the importance placed on the process, must seem impractical.

However, from the Japanese perspective, the experience and the improvement in one's spirit gained through the effort are more important than the results.

Even if the results are not good in a particular situation, one will be able to better handle future situations, thanks to the stronger spirit that one has developed.

In *bushidō*, it was thought that if one trained properly to develop the proper spiritual power, then the results would take care of themselves.

In other words, coming out ahead in a competition is nothing more than one result of the training that has been done.

□自ら by oneself
□律する discipline
□真摯に sincerely
□心がけ spirit
□重んずる highly value
□美学 aesthetic
□見受けられる one can see
□思わしくない not what are hoped for
□非合理的な impractical
□そのもの itself
□高み height
□たとえ〜としても even if
□結果は自ずとついてくる the results would take care of themselves
□〜に過ぎない nothing more than

4

気
き

Energy

気
き

14

「気」とは古代中国に生まれた概念で、この世にある目には見えないエネルギーの動きを意味します。

たとえば、会議をしているとき、お互いに意見が対立して、何も前に進まなかったとしましょう。そのとき、会議室の中になんとなく鬱々とした雰囲気が漂います。その雰囲気も「気」の一つです。

朝、澄んだ空気の中を歩いていると心が爽快になります。そんな気持ちを呼び起こす雰囲気も「気」なのです。

すなわち、「気」がよければ人は前向きで元気になり、「気」が悪ければ人は精神的にも肉体的にもくたびれてしまいます。

「気」の概念は古代の日本に伝わり、今でも日本人のものの考え方や判断の仕方に大きな影響を与えています。

「気」は場所や時間、あるいは人との関係やコミュニケーションの状況などによって様々に変化します。そして、「気」は人の心の中にもあり、その人の中によい「気」が充満していれば、仕事にも個人の生活にも充実感があるはずだと日本人は思うのです。

また、多くの場合「気」は、自分の努力で変えることができるのです。たとえば「気」が悪いと意識したら、それをよくするために何をすべきか人は考えます。会議でよい結論がでず、行き詰まったとき、休憩をとって気分転換をはかるのも、「気」を変えてよいエネルギーを呼び込む手段といえましょう。

「気」を読み取って、うまく対処できる人間が、より評価されるのです。「気配り」という概念は、まさにその時の「気」を理解して、相手に対する対応を考えることなのです。

それはロジックではありません。それゆえに文化背景の違う欧米の人にとって、「気」の概念を理解することは大変なことかも知れません。

Energy

Ki, which is a concept developed in ancient China, describes the movement of unseen energy in our world.

For example, let's say that in a meeting there is a difference of opinion that prevents the discussion from moving forward. In that situation, a depressed atmosphere will envelop the conference room. That atmosphere is an example of one type of *ki*.

When one walks in a morning's clear air, one feels refreshed. The feelings brought forth in that case are an example of another type of *ki*.

In other words, if one encounters good *ki*, one feels energetic and positive, while if one encounters bad *ki*, one feels poorly and lacks energy both spiritually and physically.

Ki has been a concept in Japan since ancient times, and today it still has a large influence on how the Japanese think and view things.

Ki will change depending on the time and place, as well as the kind of relationship of the people involved and the circumstances of their communication. *Ki* is also found in people's hearts, and the Japanese believe that if a person is full of good *ki*, then he will be fulfilled in both his work and his personal life.

In most cases, one should be able to change one's *ki* through one's own efforts. For example, if one feels that one's *ki* is not good, then one should consider in concrete terms how to improve one's *ki*. If a meeting is not progressing well, then one might consider taking a break to change the atmosphere and generate better energy.

People who are capable of gauging *ki* and handling it in an appropriate way are highly thought of. The concept of *kikubari* ("sharing one's heart"). is indeed a case of understanding the *ki* of the moment and being attuned to the needs of other people.

The concept of *ki* is not necessarily logical. For Westerners, who have grown up with a different culture, *ki* may indeed be a foreign concept.

□この世 our world
□目には見えない unseen
□なんとなく for some reason
□鬱々とした gloomy
□雰囲気が漂う an atmosphere pervades
□爽快 refreshed
□呼び起こす awaken
□前向き positive
□くたびれる get tired
□充満する fill
□充実感がある be fulfilled
□〜を意識する be aware of
□行き詰る go nowhere
□気分転換をはかる create a diversion
□手段 technique
□〜を読み取る gauge
□〜に対する be attuned to
□それゆえに therefore
□〜にとって for

運気

　「運気」とは、いわゆる占いの世界での運勢の動きを示す言葉です。西欧の占星術と同じように、中国や韓国、そして日本でも、星の動きやその人の生年月日、名前などを組み合わせた複雑な解析方法による占いが昔から存在します。

　日本人は占いが好きで、テレビのワイドショーでは今日の運勢を占うコーナーがあり、繁華街には占い師がいて、手相や姓名判断などをみてもらおうと多くの人がやってきます。

　「運気」は「気」の動きと深く関わっています。「気」の悪い状態におかれれば、その人の「運気」は下がり、やがて病気や何かのトラブルに巻き込まれるといわれています。

　「気」とは見えないエネルギーですが、それは個人の中にもあれば、宇宙の動きにも関連しています。「運気」の強い人は、そうした「気」を前向きに取り込み、自らの気力を高め、強運を導き入れることができるというわけです。

　日本には「病は気から」という言葉があります。この「気」はここで紹介する「気」のほかに、人の気持ちを示す「気」でもあるのです。つまり、精神状態がよくないと病の原因となるというのが、この言葉の意味するところです。

　心の持ち方によって、人は様々な「気」を外に発することができます。したがって、前向きに物事を考えれば、自ずと病を克服し、強い運を呼び寄せることができるというわけです。

　「運気」は自らの心の持ち方で大きく左右されるのです。

Fate

The word *unki* refers to the practice of fortune telling. Like the astrology of the West, a method of predicting one's fate based on a complex analysis of the stars or one's birthdate or name has existed in China, Korea, and Japan since ancient times.

Fortune telling is popular in Japan, with many people watching featured sections on TV shows or going to street stalls in the cities for palm reading and analysis of names.

Unki has a strong connection with the movement of *ki*. When the *ki* is not good, one's *unki* will be in a downward trend, and it is at such times that it is easy to become sick or run into trouble of some sort.

Ki is an energy that can not be seen, existing in individuals and also in connection with the movement of the universe. People with a strong fate are those who are able to take hold of that *ki* and through their own efforts pull that energy into their lives.

In Japanese the word for illness (*byōki*) is made up of the Chinese characters for "sick" (*byō*) and *ki*. In addition to the meaning of *ki* introduced here ("energy"), *ki* can also mean "feelings," as in the *ki* of *kimochi*. In other words, one's poor emotional condition may become a cause of illness.

Depending on one's emotional state, one will emit various types of *ki*. If one is in a positive state of mind, one may be able to overcome an illness on one's own and bring good luck to oneself.

One's *unki* can change significantly depending on one's attitude.

□ いわゆる so-called
□ 占い fortune telling
□ 運勢 fortune
□ 占星術 astrology
□ 生年月日 birth date
□ 組み合わせる assemble
□ 解析 analysis
□ 手相 palm reading
□ 姓名判断 fortunetelling based on writing or pronunciation of one's name
□ 関わる have a connection
□ やがて at such times
□ 前向きに positively
□ 病は気から sickness and health start with the mind
□ 発する emit
□ 克服する overcome
□ ～に左右される depend on

殺気
さっき

「気」の概念を理解するのに「殺気」は最適な概念かも知れません。

その昔、よく訓練された武士が殺意をもった相手に出会うと、相手が刀を抜いて挑みかかる前に、その殺意を感じることができたといわれていました。その殺意が空気のように漂っていることを「殺気」というのです。すなわち、言葉や明快な行動に表さなくても、そこで醸し出される雰囲気や、微妙な表情や仕草から、その人の発する「気」を読み取ることができるのです。

すでに何度か言及していますが、日本人は言葉の外にある意味を読んでコミュニケーションしようと試みます。昔、修行を重ねた武士は、相手が険しい表情をしたり、睨みつけたりという仕草をしていなくても、その人から「殺気」を感じ、心の中で闘う準備をしていたといわれています。

人の発する「気」は、相手に伝わり、相手はそれに対応して身構えることによって、自らの意思を無言で相手に伝えます。すなわち、「気」を交換することで、相対するふたりは互いに意思を伝達するのです。

現代社会において、これは漫画や映画の世界でのことですが、日本人は今でも言葉にして出すことなく、相手に気持ちを伝えようと期待することは事実です。ですから、外国の人からみれば、日本人が本当は何が言いたいのかよくわからないという戸惑いが生まれてしまうのです。

Sensing Danger

Sakki is another concept that is helpful to know in order to understand the concept of *ki*.

In the old days, it was said that a well trained samurai could sense the intent of someone to make an attempt on his life even before his opponent had drawn his sword. That sense in the air is what is known as *sakki* ("sensing danger"). In other words, even without words or clear actions, the atmosphere and subtle facial expressions or movements would allow the well trained samurai to read the *ki* of his opponent.

As we have already explained a number of times, the Japanese will try to communicate in ways other than through words. Even if his opponent were not glaring at him with a severe expression, the well-trained samurai would "sense danger" and make his mental preparations for a fight.

The *ki* one emits is sent to the person one is with, and that person in turn readies himself so that one can now send his message to the other person without using words. In other words, by exchanging *ki*, two people are able to express their wills to each other.

In the modern world, this would be the stuff of comics or movies, but it is a fact that even now the Japanese expect to be able to express their feelings to others without using words. It is because of this that non-Japanese people are puzzled and have a difficult time trying to understand what the Japanese are saying.

□その昔 in the old days
□挑みかかる attack
□殺意 intention to kill
□漂う drift about
□醸し出す engender
□雰囲気 ambience
□言及する mention
□試みる try
□険しい stern
□睨みつける glare at
□身構える stand ready
□相対する face
□期待する expect

空気
くうき

　「空気」は単に気体のことだけを意味しません。英語でも、「空気」は雰囲気など
を示すときに使われる言葉です。

　そして、日本語の場合も「空気を読む」という言葉があるように、人がコミュニ
ケーションをするにあたって、そこでの雰囲気や様子が醸し出す状況を「空気」
という言葉で表現します。

　「空気」の「空」は、何もないからっぽな状態を示す漢字です。そのからっぽな
状態に「気」が混ざり、「空気」となるのです。言葉を換えれば、「空気」は単なる
気体ではなく、そこに充満する様々なエネルギーをすべて包括したものという
ことになります。

　そこに充満しているのが、どのような「気」なのかを察知し、それをもとに適切
に物事に対処することは、日本人が常に心掛けている処世術ともいえましょう。

　したがって、「空気」の概念は、第1章で紹介した「場」とも関連します。人と
人が集まるタイミングや組み合わせによって、その場その場で様々な雰囲気が生
まれます。すなわち、「場」に充満する空気を読み、たとえば話したい話題を予定
通りに話すのか、それとも控えるのかといった判断をすることが、コミュニケー
ション上大切な戦略となるのです。

　「気」は人と人とが交流する中で生み出されるエネルギーです。したがって、
「場」や人の立場などを理解し、よりよい「気」をつくろうと多くの日本人は考え
ているのです。

Air, Atmosphere

Kūki ("air") is not simply a physical phenomenon. In English as well, "air" is also used to describe the atmosphere of a situation.

As in the Japanese phrase *kūki wo yomu* ("reading the air"), the conditions that have brought about a particular atmosphere or situation are said to be the *kūki*.

The Chinese character of *kū* in *kūki* is the character for "sky" and also means "empty." The character for *ki* is combined with the character for "sky" or "empty," to form *kūki*, or "air." Putting it another way, *kūki* is not merely a physical phenomenon; it also includes all of the various energies that inundate a particular situation.

As part of getting along in life, the Japanese will always try to determine what particular energies (*ki*) are coming to play in a situation and do their best to take appropriate action based on that.

The concept of *kūki* is therefore related to the concept of *ba* ("place") introduced in Chapter 1. Depending on the timing and combinations of when and where people get together, various types of atmosphere will be created. For example, as part of one's communication strategy, it is important to decide whether or not to bring up a particular subject based on the *kūki* of that *ba* ("place").

Ki is the energy that is created by the interchange between people. Therefore, most Japanese feel that it is important to do their best in understanding the circumstances of the people around them in order to create good *ki*.

□ 気体 gas
□ 〜にあたって upon doing
□ からっぽな empty
□ 言葉を換えれば put it another way
□ 包括する include
□ 充満する be filled with
□ 察知する determine
□ 処世術 social politics
□ その場その場で situation by situation
□ 予定通りに as planned

5

節
ふし
Period

節と節目

「型」や「道」という価値を重んずる日本人は、常に自らがどの位置にあるかを知るためのマイルストーンを大切にします。このマイルストーンを表す言葉が「節」なのです。「節」は「せつ」とも「ふし」とも読みます。

「節」とは「節目」のことで、一年の「ふしめ」である四季のことを「節」の文字を使って季節と呼んだり、人生の大きな転換期を、人生の「節目」という風に表現します。

「節目」には始まりと終わりがあります。節のコンセプトを知るために、竹をイメージしてみてください。竹には「節」があり、その成長した節が重なって、一本の竹となっています。その一本の竹を人生、あるいは何かを学ぶプロセスと考えてみると、それぞれの「節」がいかに大切で、一つ一つの「節」がなければ竹は上に伸びないことが理解できるでしょう。

「道」を極めるにあたって、この「節」の連続性がいかに保たれ、一つずつの「節」の始まりと終わりをしっかりと意識し、次の「節」につなげるかが、物事を学び、人生を送る基本であるという価値観が「節目」には込められているのです。

「節目」を重んずる日本人が、変化するときに単に未来に向かわずに、それまでお世話になった人に敬意を表したり、しっかりと挨拶をしたりすることは、欧米に人からみると、時には儀式ばってみえるかもしれません。

しかし、竹の解説からもおわかりのように、下の「節」を大切にしない限り、竹は上の「節」をつくり、伸びていかないのです。

次の始まりに向かうためにも、過去をしっかりと見つめ直すということが、「節」という概念が示す倫理観なのです。

Period

For the Japanese, who place much weight on the values of *kata* ("form") and *michi* ("way"), it is important to always take note of milestones. In Japanese, the Chinese character *setsu*, also read as *fushi*, expresses this concept of milestone.

The character of *setsu* is used with the *ki* of *shiki* ("four seasons") to make the word *kisetsu* ("season"). Again, the same character, this time read as *fushi*, is used in the word *fushime* to indicate an important transition point in a person's life.

A *fushime* ("period") has a beginning and an end. Let's use the image of bamboo to help us better understand the concept of *fushi*. A bamboo stalk has *fushi* ("nodes"), and the growth from node to node is what eventually results in a fully grown stalk. It is the same with one's life or with the process of learning something: each period is important and builds on the previous period; one cannot proceed to the next period without the last.

When seeking to master something, it is critical that continuity be preserved and that the beginning and end of each period be consciously recognized and connected with the next period, as part of the basic values of one's life. This is inherent in the concept of *fushime*.

From the point of view of Westerners, it must sometimes seem that the Japanese are simply enacting superfluous ceremonies when they mark the end of a period by going to the trouble of making various greetings and thanking people, rather than just moving on.

But for the Japanese it is a matter, of making sure that the last *fushi* is properly taken care of, like the bamboo, in order to ensure the growth of the next.

The ethics of *fushi* are clearly evident in this act of carefully considering what has happened in the past before moving on to something new.

□節目 period, turning point
□転換期 transition point
□〜という風に like this
□竹 bamboo
□連続性 continuity
□物事 things
□人生を送る live a life
□込められている be embedded in
□お世話になる be indebted to someone
□儀式ばってみえる ceremonious looking
□おわかりのように as you can see
□〜しない限り unless one does
□倫理観 ethical sense

有終
ゆうしゅう

　「有終」とは終わりをしっかりと意識するという価値観です。多くの場合、「節」あるいは「節目」に示される倫理観を最も端的に表した言葉が、「有終の美」です。

　たとえば、会社を辞めて、次のチャンスに向けて旅立つとき、人はまさに「節目」を経験します。その「節目」を大切にして、未来へ向かうために、辞めていく会社で最後の日までしっかりと働きます。そしてお世話になった人への挨拶を忘れず、**後任に引き継ぎ**をして、時には自分の机や周囲の掃除までして会社を去ることが、「有終の美」の価値観なのです。

　この考え方は日常生活でもみることができます。ホテルや旅館に宿泊したとき、旅立つ前に部屋や布団を**簡単に**片付けたりする**行為**も「有終の美」の一例です。

　「**立つ鳥跡を濁さず**」ということわざがあります。これは、水鳥は**飛び立つ**とき池を濁すことなくきれいに飛び立つという意味から、旅立つとき、またはその場を去るとき、後の人のためにもその場所を美しく保って去ってゆこうということを意味します。

　「有終の美」は、このことわざにもつながる、過去から未来への人や社会の繋がりをしっかりと意識するための倫理観といえるのではないでしょうか。

Beautiful Ending

The word *yūshū* expresses the social value of coming to terms with an ending. In many cases, the ethical values of *fushi* or *fushime* can be expressed most directly in the phrase *yūshū no bi* ("beautiful ending").

For example, when a person quits his job and moves on to his next opportunity, he is clearly experiencing a *fushime* ("transition point"). "A beautiful ending" can be seen in this case, as the person treats the transition with respect, working hard up through the last day, making proper greetings to his colleagues, briefing his replacement, and even in the way he cleans out his desk before leaving his job.

We can also see this way of thinking in everyday life. Tidying up the room and putting the futon away before leaving a hotel or Japanese inn would be another example of a "beautiful ending."

There is a saying in Japan that "a bird taking off doesn't muddy the waters." In the same way that a water bird takes flight from a pond without disturbing the water, so should a person, be careful to put things in order so as not to inconvenience those left behind.

The ethical sense behind a "beautiful ending" is also seen in this saying, as one properly connects the people and events of one's past with one's future.

□ 端的に表わす express simply
□ 有終の美 beautiful ending
□ 辞める resign
□ 後任 replacement
□ 引き継ぎ taking over charge
□ 簡単に shortly
□ 行為 act
□ ～を濁す muddy
□ ことわざ saying
□ 飛び立つ take flight

節度
_{せつど}

20

竹の「節」の一つ一つを人生になぞらえ、大切に生きてゆこうという発想は、自らが現在留まっている「節」の中で、自分を整え、その「節」を破ることなく、次の「節」に旅立つまでしっかりと謙虚に自分を磨こうという価値観を導きます。その価値観を「節度」と呼びます。「和」の章でみてきた、「謙遜」や「謙譲」という価値観が融合して「節度」という意識となってここで活きてくるのです。

敢えて自らを強くアピールすることなく、現在おかれている位置や立場を理解し、その日々の積み重ねから自身が成長してゆくことが「節度」という価値観です。

ダイナミックに変化する現代において、封建時代から培われてきたこの価値観は時代にそぐわないかもしれません。

よく、日本人は何を考え、何がしたいのかわからないという苦情を（外国の人から）聞きますが、その背景には、日本人が常に「節度」という価値観を持ち、自らの考えや思いを強く主張することを控えようという意識があるからかもしれません。

しかし、「節度」という価値観のよい面は、常に人に対して感謝や尊敬の念をもって接する心構えでしょう。

現代のビジネス社会において、いかにチームワークをもってプロジェクトを進めてゆくかというテーマは大切です。そのとき、相手の立場を考え、相手に敬意を表しながら「節度」あるアプローチをとれば、多くの場合、対立がシナジーへと変化するかもしれません。

価値観は古くなるのでも、的はずれになるのでもありません。むしろ、価値観にとらわれ形骸化した行動が、価値観そのものを古くさくしてしまうのです。

そうした意味では、「節度」という価値観のよい面を見直してみるのも、必要なのではないでしょうか。

Restraint

Just as each node in a bamboo stalk is like each period in one's life, so it is that one must also do the utmost to train and prepare oneself while one is in a particular period of life, while also being careful not to go on to the next stage before one is ready. This value is called *setsudo* ("restraint"). In the chapter on *wa* ("harmony"), we discussed the value of modesty (*kenson*, *kenjō*), and here we will see how modesty is reflected in the concept of *setsudo*.

Rather than seeking individual recognition, *setsudo* means working hard day-to-day to improve oneself within one's current position and situation.

This value, which has been cultivated in Japan since feudal times, may not fit with today's world, in which dynamic change is the norm.

Non-Japanese may often complain that they don't know what the Japanese are thinking or what they want to do. *Setsudo* may be behind this, as the Japanese will refrain from giving strong opinions with this value in mind.

On the other hand, the good aspects of *setsudo* are the gratitude and respect always paid to other people.

In today's business world, the amount of teamwork that can be brought to bear on a project is very important. If an approach employing *setsudo* is used, one in which the position of other people is carefully considered and the proper respect is paid to them, then in a surprisingly large number of cases it may be possible to change conflict into synergy.

It is not a matter of values becoming old and irrelevant on their own. Rather, it is a matter of the essence of values being lost due to the changing attitudes and actions of people.

In that sense, it may be necessary to acknowledge once again the good aspects of *setsudo*.

☐ 発想 idea

☐ 現在留まっている currently staying

☐ 自分を整える get yourself in order

☐ 謙虚 humility, modesty

☐ 導く lead

☐ 融合する blend

☐ 活きてくる be in effect

☐ 積み重ね buildup

☐ そぐわない not fit with

☐ 苦情 complaint

☐ よい面 good aspect

☐ 尊敬の念 a sense of respect

☐ 接する contact

☐ テーマ theme

☐ アプローチをとる approach

☐ シナジー synergy

☐ 的はずれ irrelevant

☐ 形骸化する become a mere shell

☐ 古くさくする make ~ outdated

けじめ

21

「有終の美」の概念でもおわかりのように、日本人は一見非合理的にすら見えるほどに、物事の終わりを大切にし、「節目」をしっかりと意識しながら未来へ向かうことをよしとします。

この物事の変化にあたって、しっかりと「節」の価値観に従って行動することを日本人は「けじめ」といいます。

たとえば、人が罪を犯した場合、ただ逃げ隠れするのではなく、あえて警察に自首し、刑に服することがあります。この行為を日本では、「けじめ」をつけるといいます。すなわち、自らの行動に対してしっかりと責任をとり、それにふさわしい態度や対応をすることが「けじめ」なのです。

現在でも、日本人は「けじめ」を常に意識しているようです。

たとえば、ビジネスの世界で、会社が不良品を製造したり、業績が低迷したりという厳しい状態におかれたとき、日本では会社の経営者が責任をとって辞任することが頻繁にあります。直接その人が原因で起きた問題でなくとも、責任者として、会社が未来へ向かうための「けじめ」をつけるのです。

物事が変化する節目に、いかに「けじめ」をつけるか。日本人はそこでの行動に注目して、その人物を評価するわけです。

Marking a Break

As seen in the concept of *yūshū no bi* ("a beautiful ending"), the Japanese can appear impractical in how they treat endings, taking due note of *fushime* ("transition points") before moving on to a new stage of life.

Kejime is the action one takes in accord with the concept of *fushi* ("period") as one marks a change in one's life.

For example, if one commits a crime and, instead of running away, one turns oneself into the police and submits to the appropriate punishment, in Japan this is called *kejime wo tsukeru* ("marking a break"). In other words, having the right attitude to take responsibility for one's actions is an important aspect of *kejime*.

The Japanese today remain very aware of the concept of *kejime*.

For example, it is quite common in Japan for the chief executive of a company to resign if his company has manufactured and sold defective goods. Even if the executive was not the direct cause of the defective goods, as the head of the company, it is incumbent on him to "mark a break" (*kejime wo tsukeru*) and take responsibility. For the Japanese, a person will be judged on how sincerely he "marks the break" during such a transition point (*fushime*) in his life.

□非合理的 impractical
□〜にすら見える can appear to be
□罪を犯す commit a crime
□逃げ隠れする run away and then hide oneself
□自首する turn oneself into the police
□刑に服する submit to the punishment
□業績 performance
□低迷する hover at a low level
□〜の責任を取って辞任する step down to take responsibility for
□頻繁に frequently
□〜でなくとも even if it is not
□責任者 responsible person
□評価する evaluate

6

情
じょう
Feelings

情
じょう

22

「情」とは人の思いや感情を表す漢字です。

人の喜びや悲しみ、楽しみや苦しみを生み出す心のエネルギーを、日本人は「情」という言葉で言い表すのです。

よく、欧米の人が、日本の映画やテレビドラマは、**感情 表現の場がしつこく、ウエットすぎる**と批判します。その一つの理由として、日本人はジェスチャーや言葉を使って、感情を強く表現しないため、どうしても感情 表現の場が長くなってしまうことが挙げられます。

恋人同士の別れの場を表現するときに、「愛しているよ。またすぐ逢いたい」と言えばすむ場面を、じっと涙をこらえて、**目頭がすこし潤んできたときに、恋人を乗せた列車が出発する**というように、むしろ**言葉を交えずに表現**したほうが、日本人の心に響いてくるのです。

特に、言葉は**できるだけ少ない方が、説得力がある**とするコミュニケーションスタイルをもつ日本人にとっては、言葉に表さない「情」を知覚することが、相手を理解する大切な**要因**となるのです。

このコミュニケーションスタイルが、日本人特有の「情」への価値観を育みました。すなわち、「情」は言葉に表さない人間の気持ちへの美学によって支えられた価値観なのです。

日本人は、「情」を感じるとき、相手に対して何かしてあげなければというモチベーションを抱きます。そうしたモチベーションへの期待が、日本人特有の人間関係における**紐帯を育む**わけです。そしてビジネスであろうが個人であろうが、「情」を感じ合うとき、お互いに**打ち解け合って**話ができるのです。日本人特有の身近な人への**甘えの構造**がそこに見えてくるのです。

70

情

Feelings

Jō is the Chinese character for "feelings."

The Japanese express the energy created by such emotions as happiness, sadness, pleasure, and distress in the word *jō*.

Westerners often criticize Japanese movies or television dramas for being too emotional. One reason that can be given for this is that the Japanese tend to express their emotions indirectly rather than by using a lot of words or gestures; this means that it takes longer for such emotional scenes to be played out.

When two lovers part at a train station, for example, rather than simply saying, "I love you; I want to see you again soon," it is more emotional for the Japanese to play out the scene without words, with tears slowly building in the eyes and then trickling down the cheeks as the train leaves.

Particularly for the Japanese, whose communication style uses as few words as possible, it is critical when trying to understand another person to grasp the *jō* that is being expressed nonverbally.

It is this communication style that brought about the Japanese value of *jō*. In other words, it is the beauty of nonverbal human emotions that brings true life to this value.

When the Japanese feel *jō*, that is when they are most motivated to act. It is in turn this motivation to act, generated by *jō*, which creates the bonds of *ningen kankei* ("human relationships"), which are so important to the Japanese. It is here, too, that one can see the concept of *amae* ("dependency") in relationships with those to whom one is close.

□ 感情表現 an emotional expression
□ 場 scene
□ しつこい persistent
□ ウェットすぎる too emotional
□ どうしても unavoidably
□ 逢う meet
□ じっと quietly
□ 目頭 inner corner of one's eye
□ 潤む be wet, be moist
□ 言葉を交えず without using words
□ できるだけ少ない as few as possible
□ 説得力がある eloquent
□ ～を知覚する perceive
□ 要因 factor
□ ～を抱く hold
□ 紐帯を育む create the bonds
□ AであろうがBであろうが whether A or B
□ 打ち解け合って confidentially
□ 甘えの構造 pampering structure

人情

23

「情」という価値観をもっと端的に示しているのが「人情」という価値観です。洋の東西を問わず、人は誰でも親しい人に対して**愛情を抱いています**。また、めぐまれない人に接すれば、たいていの人には**同情心**がうまれます。この、他の人に対する個人的な感情を「人情」といいます。

たとえば、**刑事裁判**で、被告人が不幸な**境遇**にあった**がために罪を犯した**であろうと思われる場合、判事が軽い**判決を下す**ことがあります。この場合、判事は「人情」によって心を動かされたとされ、人々はその判決に**拍手する**というわけです。

こうした話はよく**時代劇**の題材になります。「人情」によってビジネスや **公**の決裁が影響を受けることは、日本ではむしろよいこととされているのです。状況によっては、「情」を加えることはむしろプラスなのです。

実は、日本人は、「ビジネスはビジネス」として、個人の「情」とビジネスを切り離すべきものだという考えになかなか**馴染めません**。本来は客観的に意見を交換し、判断を行うべきビジネスでのやりとりが、日本では「ハートとハート」のやりとりとして受け取られ、**それがもとで**人間関係が上手くいかなくなったり、取引が**不調におわる**こともあるのです。

もちろん、日本でもビジネスと個人の「情」とを**混同**してはいけないという道徳律は存在します。それだけに、人は反対意見を**述べ**たりするときは、「人情」を意識し、気を使い、相手の**立場をたて**ながら**表明**するのです。

その表明の仕方**自体**が、欧米の人からみると、ビジネスと個人の「情」とが混在しているようにみえることもあるようです。

Personal Feelings

Ninjō is the value of *jō* ("feelings") expressed in a more direct manner. It is the willingness to embrace the love of all people without question as to their nationality. It also means that there is a sympathy for those whom one comes into contact with who have not been so fortunate in their lives. These emotions that one has for others are called *ninjō*.

For example, if a court is trying a criminal, the judge may give a lighter sentence if the person in question committed the crime due to the unfortunate circumstances of his environment. In that case, it would be said that the judge had been moved by *ninjō* and people would applaud his decision.

This type of story is often seen in *jidai geki* ("samurai tales"). In other words, when *ninjō* moves a person to be generous in making a business or public service decision, this is considered a good thing in Japan; and depending on the situation, the more generous the better.

It is true that it is difficult for most Japanese to accept the idea that "business is business" and separate their personal feelings from business. Although business should be conducted in a manner in which ideas are objectively exchanged and judgments made on that basis, in Japan it is instead common to conduct business on a "heart-to-heart basis," and this can often lead to broken relationships and bad business deals.

Of course in Japan, the principle of not mixing business with one's personal feelings also exists. When one is faced with someone taking an opposing position, however, one takes *ninjō* into account and is careful to do what one can to accommodate that person.

It is this very tendency of Japanese to take *ninjō* into account in such cases that apparently leads Westerners to believe that Japanese are mixing business and their personal feelings.

□ 洋の東西を問わず regardless of their origin
□ 愛情を抱く fix one's affection on
□ めぐまれない not been so fortunate
□ たいていの most
□ 同情心 sympathy
□ 刑事裁判 criminal trial
□ 境遇 circumstances
□ 〜がために due to
□ 判決を下す pass judgment
□ 拍手する applaud
□ 時代劇 samurai drama
□ 公の決裁 official decision
□ 馴染む accept
□ それがもとで because of that
□ 不調におわる lead bad business deals
□ 混同する mix up
□ それだけに for that reason
□ 述べる state
□ 立場をたてる show respect to someone's situation
□ 〜自体 itself

義理

24

　「義理」とは、人と人とが人間関係を維持してゆくための義務や務めを意味する言葉です。

　たとえば、ある人に大変お世話になった場合、その人に対して「義理」があると人はいいます。そこで生まれる義理を意識して、受けた恩恵に報いることが道徳的に求められているわけです。

　日本の場合、この人と人との縛りが伝統的に強かったといえましょう。特に、江戸時代に代表される封建時代には、身分や性別、そして年齢など、様々な立場での役割が厳しく設定されていました。そして、役割を逸脱することや、自らの立場を超えて行動することは禁じられていたのです。

　したがって、「義理」に縛られながら、その縛りを超えた人と人の「情」との間に挟まれて葛藤するテーマが、歌舞伎や文楽などの伝統芸能でよく取り上げられました。たとえば、親の「義理」に縛られて婚約させられた娘と、その娘に恋する若者の物語などが、それにあたります。「義理」と「人情」というテーマです。

　ごく日常的な「義理」といえば、夏や年の暮れに、仕事上あるいはふだんの付き合いでお世話になった人に贈り物をしたり、挨拶にいったりする習慣があります。今でこそ少なくなりましたが、上司が引っ越しをするときに、部下がそれを手伝うといった習慣も挙げられます。

　多くの場合、「義理」はこうした上下関係での道徳律と深く関わっています。上司にお酒に誘われて、恋人とのデートの約束をどうしようかと迷うのも、現代版の「義理」と「人情」といえましょう。

　最近は、こうした場合、若い人は「人情」を優先すると、年輩の人はぼやいているのもまた事実なのです。

74

Obligation, Duty

Giri means the responsibility and effort that go into maintaining a relationship between one person and another.

For example, if one is indebted to another for a favor done, then it is said that one has *giri* to the other person. In that case, Japanese ethics require that one be well aware of the *giri* incurred and repay the favor.

In Japan this type of connection from person to person has traditionally been strong. Especially during the feudal Edo Era, one's position was strictly fixed according to one's rank, sex, age, and so on. It was not possible to deviate from one's rank or make an attempt to better oneself within society.

Because of this, conflicts between one's obligations (*giri*) and one's feelings (*ninjō*) were a common theme in the traditional performing arts such as the *kabuki* or *bunraku* ("puppet theatre"). An example of such a conflict would be a daughter who became engaged to one man to fulfill her *giri* to her father, while her true affections (*ninjō*) were for another young man. This would be a classic *giri-ninjō* theme.

In terms of everyday life, an example of *giri* would be giving gifts and making the rounds of greetings during the summer and at the end of the year to those whom one is indebted to for social or business favors. Another example, which is rare nowadays, would be for subordinates in a company to help their boss move.

As in these cases, *giri* often has a strong connection to the ethics of relationships between those in higher and lower positions. It might be said that a modern version of a *giri-ninjō* conflict would be for a boss to invite one out for a drink on a night when one already had a date set with one's girlfriend.

It is a fact that older people today are not happy with the way that younger people tend to put *ninjō* ahead of *giri*.

□ 維持する maintain
□ 義務や務め obligations and duties
□ 恩恵 benefit
□ 報いる repay
□ 人と人との縛り connection between people
□ 江戸時代 Edo Era (1603-1868)
□ 役割 role
□ 逸脱する deviate
□ 葛藤する undergo a conflict
□ 伝統芸能 traditional performing arts
□ 年の暮れに at the end of the year
□ 習慣 custom
□ 今でこそ nowadays
□ 上下関係 hierarchical relationship
□ 現代版 modern version
□ Aを(Bより)優先する put A ahead of B
□ 年輩の人 older people
□ ぼやく grumble

恩
おん

25

「義理」という考え方に最も影響を与えるのが「恩」という価値観です。

封建時代には、君主は自らの部下である侍に俸禄を与え、その侍の身分を保障します。その地位は、その侍一代ではなく、代々受け継がれることが普通でした。

この身分と生活の保障を君主から受けることが、侍にとっての「恩」です。侍はその受けている「恩」に報いるために、時には命をかけて君主に仕えなければなりません。すなわちそれが侍の「義理」というわけです。

現在でも、「あの人には恩がある」と人はよくいいます。自分を育ててくれた親への「恩」、知識を与えてくれた教師への「恩」、そしてスキルを教えてくれた上司への「恩」などがそれにあたります。

人は「恩」に対して、それに報いるように努力することが求められます。「恩」と「義理」との関係は、一時的なものではなく、多くの場合一生その人の人間関係に影響を与えます。昔は「恩」を忘れることは、最も非道徳的なこととして、非難されていたのです。

日本人の心の中に深く残る「恩」という発想は、日本人がビジネスの上でも単にビジネスライクに物事を進めるのではなく、個人的な感情で判断をする原因の一つにもなっています。たとえば、「恩」のある人の子供だからということで、昇進や就職に手を加えることも時にはあり、それが様々な不正の原因となることもあるのです。

逆に、あの人には「恩」があるからということで、その人が死んだ後も、その子供や遺族の相談にのろうとする行為は、美徳であるともいえるでしょう。

「恩」という発想には、こうした功罪両面があるようです。

Social Debt

The social value known as *on* has heavily influenced the concept of *giri* ("obligation").

In the feudal period, a lord would pay his samurai a stipend and guarantee their position in society. It was the usual practice to guarantee that rank not just to that particular samurai, but to his descendants as well.

Having received a position and the guarantee of a living, the samurai would have incurred *on*, and in order to repay that social debt, the samurai would loyally serve his lord, at times having to put his life on the line. In other words, this was the samurai's *giri* ("obligation").

Even today, people often speak of "having *on*" to a particular person. Common examples would be the *on* that is incurred by a child to his parent, or a student to his teacher, or an employee to his boss.

It is expected that those who incur *on* will make efforts to repay it. In most cases, *on* and *giri* are lifelong obligations, not something which affects one only for the short-term. In the old days, forgetting to repay one's *on* was considered a very unethical act and would be heavily criticized.

The concept of *on*, which is so deeply rooted in the character of the Japanese, is one reason why they are not able to take a more "business-like" approach to business, instead allowing personal feelings to affect their judgments. For example, inequities often result from giving favorable consideration for hiring or promotion to the child of someone to whom one has incurred *on*.

On the other hand, it is a thing of beauty to see someone reach out to assist the child or other family members of someone to whom one has incurred *on* after that person has died.

In this way, the concept of *on* would appear to have both merits and demerits.

☐ 君主 lord
☐ 俸禄 stipend
☐ 保障する guarantee
☐ 一代 one lifetime
☐ 代々受け継がれる handed down from generation to generation
☐ 恩に報いる repay a favor
☐ 一時的な temporary
☐ 一生 lifelong
☐ 非道徳的な unethical
☐ 非難される be criticized
☐ 深く残る be deeply rooted
☐ 昇進 promotion
☐ 手を加える give favorable consideration
☐ 相談にのる provide consultation
☐ 功罪両面 both merits and demerits

情

内と外

26

人と人との複雑なしがらみの中で、その人の「情」と「義理」との関係がわかり、**心を許して**話ができる信頼関係が構築されたとき、その人は自分の人間関係の「内」にいると考えられます。

たとえば、家族や会社の親しい同僚は「内」の関係で、そこに入らない人は「外」の人と**捉えられます**。「外」の人とは、**ある程度**お互いがよく知り合うまで、率直な付き合いを控えるのです。

この「内」と「外」との**境界線**は、その人のおかれている**立ち位置**の違いによって変化します。たとえば、同じ村の人でも、家族からみると「外」の人ですが、違う村の人と比較すれば、「内」の人となります。外国の人を「外人」と呼びますが、この場合は日本を「内」と捉えているので、外国は「外」に**他ならない**のです。すなわち、「外人」とは「外の人」という意味なのです。

複雑な人間関係から発生する**齟齬**や**軋轢**といったリスク**を軽減する**ために、日本人は伝統的に「内」と考える相手**に対してのみ**、本当の思いや情報を共有する**傾向にあります**。

「内」に迎えられるためには、何よりも、お互いを**公私ともに**よく知り合う必要があります。そして、「情」をもって話し合える関係になれば、「内」に入った仲間として情報が共有されるのです。

日本人がビジネスの関係においても、よく夕食を共にし、お酒を飲んで騒いだりする背景には、お互いに「内」の関係になろうとする**意識が働いている**のです。これは、外国人のように日本社会の「内」に入りにくい人にとっては、常に**お客さ**んとして扱われ、親切には**されるものの**、**打ち解ける**ことができないという問題に**直面する**リスクもあるのです。

日本で、「内」に迎えられるためには、まずビジネスライクな付き合いをやめて、プライベートな話を**共有し**、一緒に過ごす時間を増やしてゆく努力が必要なのかもしれません。

Inside and Outside, Social Circle

When one is able to navigate the *shigarami* ("barriers") of a relationship and understand the particulars of *jō* ("feelings") versus *giri* ("obligations") to the point that one can let one's guard down and truly trust that person, then it is said that that person is *uchi* ("inside").

For example, a person who is not within one's family or close associates at one's company would be considered to be *soto* ("outside"), and one would have some reserve in dealing with that person until one got to know the person better.

How to distinguish between *uchi* and *soto* depends on the situation in question. For example, people in the same village who are not in the same family would be considered *soto* in terms of family, but those same people would be considered *uchi* in terms of the village versus people from outside the village. In Japanese, a foreigner is literally called *soto no hito* or *gaijin* ("outside person"). In this case, if we take Japan to be *uchi* ("inside"), then foreign countries must be seen as *soto* ("outside").

To reduce the risk of dealing with the complications of relationships, the Japanese have traditionally tended to only really open up to share information and personal feelings with people whom they felt were *uchi* ("inside") their social circle.

In order to be welcomed "inside" (*uchi*), it is necessary that two persons know each other well both publicly and privately. Then they will be in a position where they can open up to their feelings (*jō*) as persons "inside" the same social circle and freely share information.

In terms of business, it is common for Japanese to have dinner and drinks together as they attempt to build a relationship in which they can both be "inside." For foreigners, who may find it difficult to break into the social circle, there is the risk that they will continue to be treated politely as guests without being able to get their Japanese counterparts to open up to them.

In order to be welcomed "inside" in Japan, it is necessary to not have a purely "business-like" relationship and instead to be sure to increase the time spent in sharing private interests.

□ しがらみ ties of obligation
□ 心を許す let one's guard down
□ 捉える consider
□ ある程度 to some extent
□ 率直な frank
□ 境界線 boundary
□ 立ち位置 position
□ 〜に他ならない must be
□ 齟齬 contradiction
□ 軋轢 friction
□ 〜を軽減する reduce
□ 〜に対してのみ only for
□ 〜する傾向にある tend to
□ 公私ともに publicly and privately
□ 意識が働く attempt to do
□ お客さん guest
□ 〜ではあるものの although
□ 打ち解ける open up
□ 直面する confront
□ 共有する share

本音と建前

27

「内」と「外」との関係を最も象徴的に表した言葉が、「本音」と「建前」です。「本音」とは、「内」の同じグループのメンバー同士で語られる本当に思っている内容のことで、「建前」は、表向きの、あるいは外交的なメッセージや言葉を指す表現となります。

日本人ならではのコミュニケーションスタイルを理解している人同士であれば、「本音」と「建前」とを見分けることは比較的簡単かもしれません。しかし、外国から来た人は、「建前」を聞いて、それを「本音」と勘違いし、あとになって思うように事が進まずにびっくりすることもしょっちゅうあります。残念なことに、この「本音」と「建前」を理解していない人から見れば、あたかも日本人が嘘をついているように誤解することもあるかもしれません。

日本人から「本音」のメッセージを受け取るには、「内」に入ること、あるいは相手の属する「内」に加わる人を通して間接的に情報をとることが求められます。そして、何よりも、そうした人を介して相手を夕食などに招待し、お酒を酌み交わしながら、打ち解けてゆくことも大切です。

「本音」と「建前」は、外国の人にとって、最もやっかいな日本人のコミュニケーションスタイルのひとつなのです。

True Feelings and Facade

Two words that most closely represent the relationship of *uchi* ("inside") and *soto* ("outside") are *honne* and *tatemae*. *Honne* refers to the true feelings that are spoken by those who are "inside" (*uchi*) the same group, while *tatemae* is what is spoken for show or to be diplomatic.

For those who understand the Japanese communication style, it is relatively easy to see the difference between what is *honne* and what is *tatemae*. However, it is quite common for non-Japanese people to hear what is *tatemae* and misunderstand it as *honne*, later being surprised when things don't progress as they had thought they would. Unfortunately for those who cannot tell the difference between *honne* and *tatemae*, misunderstandings may sometimes arise where it is felt that the Japanese are not telling the truth.

In order to get the true intent (*honne*) of a Japanese person, one will be expected to become a member of his "inside" (*uchi*) group or go through someone who is inside the group. Above all else, it is then important to take that person out to dinner and have a few drinks with him in order to get him to fully open up.

For the foreigner, understanding *honne* and *tatemae* may be one of the most challenging aspects of the Japanese communication style.

□ 象徴的に figuratively
□ 表向きの for show
□ 〜ならではの special to
□ 見分ける see the difference
□ 比較的 relatively
□ 勘違いする misunderstand
□ 思うように as one had thought one would
□ しょっちゅう quite common
□ 残念なことに unfortunately
□ あたかも as if
□ 属する be part of
□ 加わる人 participant
□ 〜を通して［介して］through
□ 間接的に indirectly
□ 何よりも above all else
□ 酌み交わす drink together
□ やっかいな challenging

7

忠
ちゅう

Loyalty

忠
ちゅう

28

前章の「恩」の概念を思い出してください。

人から「恩」を受けると、**それに対する**「義理」が発生します。

「忠」は、その「義理」の中でも特に**身分や立場の高い人に対して発生する義務**を示す言葉です。

「恩」を与えてくれた人に対して、しっかりと敬意を表し、行動をもってその人に対して**尽くしてゆく**考え方が「忠」です。したがって、「忠」という概念は、より身分の上下がはっきりしていた封建時代において特に強調された**道徳的規範**であり、そこから**派生する行動規範**となるのです。

現代社会において、「忠」という意識をそのまま**強要される**ことは少なくなりました。しかし、会社に対して**忠誠心**を持ち、時には**自らを犠牲にしても会社の**ために**労苦を惜しまず**仕事をするという美学が、今でも日本社会には残っています。「忠」という意識は、日本人の心の奥深くに**刻まれている遺伝子のようなもの**なのかもしれません。

Loyalty

Please recall our discussion of *on* ("debt" or "favor") in the last chapter.

One receives *on* from someone, and in turn one incurs *giri* (an "obligation").

Within the concept of *giri*, *chū* is the particular type of obligation that is incurred to someone of high rank or position.

The concept of *chū* means respecting and serving a person from whom one has received *on*. In the feudal period, when rank and position were even more clearly defined, the ethical norms of *chū* were therefore all the more emphasized.

In today's modern society, the awareness per se of *chū* is not as strong as it once was. However, even today in Japan, people will have loyalty to their company and from time to time sacrifice themselves by taking on undesirable assignments for the greater good of the company. It may be that this sense of *chū* ("loyalty") is grafted deeply into the DNA of the Japanese.

□ それに対する in turn
□ 身分 status
□ 立場の高い人 someone of high rank
□ 尽くしてゆく devote oneself
□ 道徳的規範 ethical norm
□ 派生する derive
□ 行動規範 code of conduct
□ 強要される be forced
□ 忠誠心 loyalty
□ 自らを犠牲にする sacrifice oneself
□ 労苦を惜しまず painstakingly
□ 刻む etch
□ 遺伝子 gene
□ 〜のようなもの kind of

上下
じょうげ

29

「上」と「下」の概念は、「忠」と大変深く関わっています。

今はもちろん存在しませんが、封建時代には、身分の「上下」が社会制度の基本でした。特に士農工商という４つの身分に人は分けられ、武士が最も高く、商人は最も低い地位にありました。そしてたとえば武士の中でも、幾層にも身分が分かれていたのです。

この身分の「上下」という考え方は、現代社会では、たとえば上司と部下、先生と生徒の間でみられます。あるいは生け花や茶道の学習にみられる家元制度などに強く受け継がれています。産業によっては、官と民間の間にも、大企業とその下請けの間にも、上下の意識が歴然と残っています。

日本では、相手の人格が自らより「上」の立場にあるか、「下」にあるかによって、言葉遣いも変われば、応対も違ってきます。

もちろん、欧米でも立場の「上下」はあり、相手がどういう立場かによって、ある程度は応対を変える習慣はあります。しかし、人と人とは基本的に平等で、挨拶の方法にそれほどの変化があるわけではありません。

しかし、日本では「上下」関係の「義理」に縛られた行動様式が、欧米よりも際立っていることは否めないようです。

もちろん、法律的にも制度の上でも、「上下」による差別は日本でも違法行為です。しかし、「上下」に関する人の意識は法的な規制とは別に、日本社会の根本原理として維持されているのです。

Hierarchy

The concept of "higher" rank and "lower" rank strongly influences *chū* ("loyalty").

During the feudal period, there was a strict system of hierarchy, although such a class system does not of course exist today. At that time, society was split into four classes: samurai, farmer, craftsman, and merchant, with the samurai at the top and the merchant at the bottom. Within the samurai class, there were several additional distinctions of rank.

In Japan today, *jōge* can still be seen in the relationship between boss and subordinate, or between teacher and student. It is also still very much alive in the disciplines of flower arrangement and the tea ceremony, for example. Depending on the industry, there may be *jōge* relationships in place between government agencies and private companies; and clearly a *jōge* relationship can be seen between large companies and their subcontractors.

In Japan, one's language and the way one interacts with another person will differ depending on whether the other person is "higher" or "lower" than oneself. For Westerners as well, the concept of "hierarchy" exists and the way one person greets another will differ to some degree depending on the status of the other person. In principle, however, people are treated as equals, and there is not as large a difference.

In Japan, however, it cannot be denied that the concept of *jōge* plays a greater role than it does in the West, due to the way in which *giri* ("obligation") strongly affects actions.

Of course, in Japan as well today, discrimination based on *jōge* is against the law. That said, the concept of *jōge* is still deeply rooted in Japanese society.

□ 士農工商 four-tiered class system
□ 商人 merchant
□ 地位 position
□ 幾層にも several additional
□ 生け花 flower arrangement
□ 茶道 tea ceremony
□ 家元制度 hereditary headmastership system
□ 官と民間 government agencies and private companies
□ 下請け subcontractor
□ 歴然と clearly
□ 人格 personality
□ 言葉遣い use of language
□ 応対 response
□ それほどの(〜ではない) not as large as
□ 行動様式 mode of behavior
□ 際立っている outstanding
□ 否めない it cannot be denied
□ 違法行為 illegal activity
□ 法的な規制 legal restrictions
□ 根本原理 fundamental principle

奉公 (ほうこう)

30

封建時代に「恩」を受けた人に期待される行動が「奉公」でした。

この「恩」と「奉公」との関係は、単にビジネスライクなものではありません。侍は、その一生、さらにその祖先から子孫へと、君主や上司から「恩」を受け、それに対する「義理」として「奉公」するわけですから、その紐帯は深く、単なる人間関係を超えた「情」と「義理」とで結ばれたものでした。

滅私奉公という言葉があります。その意味するところは、私情に左右されず、「恩」を受けた人に対してとことん仕えるという倫理観を示しています。時には、自らの命を捧げて君主を守り、その行為に対して君主は、その人物の家族や子孫へもさらなる利益を与えてゆくのです。こうしてこの滅私奉公という、ある意味自己犠牲の考え方は正当化されるのです。

滅私奉公をすることによって、人は「恩」を与える者に対する「情」の深さを示し、その「情」によって気持ちを動かされた上に立つ者は、さらに「奉公」する者に愛情を注ぐのです。

このプロセスの名残が、現代社会にもあります。個人の予定よりも会社や上司のニーズを優先して残業をする意識など、一見過去の価値観と思われがちな「奉公」という意識が、現在の日本人にも受け継がれ、大切な価値観となっていることには驚かされます。

Service

During the feudal period, it was expected that *on* ("social debt") would be repaid through *hōkō* ("service").

This relationship of *on* and *hōkō* was not simply a business arrangement. For a samurai, the *on* that was incurred extended throughout his own life and stretched back to his grandfather and forward to his grandchildren, resulting in a deep bond with his lord that was based on *jō* ("feelings") and *giri* ("obligation").

Messhi hōkō ("self-sacrificing service"), is an expression that means to not be swayed by personal feelings in repaying through service the *on* that one has incurred. On occasion a samurai would have to give up his life in order to protect his lord, and in turn the lord would grant additional benefits to that samurai's family and descendants; in this way there would be compensation for the sacrifice (*messhi hōkō*) of the samurai.

Through one's service, a person shows the depth of his feelings (*jō*) towards the person to whom he has incurred *on* ("social debt"), and in turn that person will be further moved and show his affection for the person providing the service.

The product of this process continues to be found in Japan today. To a surprising degree, the values of *hōkō*, which had been thought to be old and passé, have continued on—in the way a Japanese will work overtime to put the needs of his boss or the company before his personal ambitions, for example.

□期待される expected

□紐帯 relationship

□滅私奉公 self-sacrificing service

□左右される be swayed by

□とことん completely

□命を捧げる give up one's life

□さらなる additional

□ある意味 in a way

□正当化する be justified

□上に立つ者 superior

□名残 vestige

□一見 seemingly

□〜(し)がちな prone to

忠義

31

　武士の社会では「奉公」という概念を、特に「忠義」という考え方に**結びつけて**いました。「忠義」は、武士が自らの主君に対して**命をかけて**「奉公」することを示す言葉です。

　「忠義」は「**武士道**」の**根本**を**貫く**ストイックな精神で、主君を守るために死の恐怖をも克服して忠誠を保つことを侍に要求している**価値観**です。

　したがって、武士は徹底的に「忠義」を尽すことが美徳とされ、そのために常に精神的な**修養**と、武道の**稽古**、学問の**研鑽**が求められていたのです。

　「奉公」の概念が、武士に限らずより一般的に、「恩」に報いるための行為を示しているのに対し、「忠義」は武士が「奉公」するための意識を表す言葉として、彼らの倫理的な**核**となった言葉です。

　忠臣蔵という日本人なら誰でも知っている物語があります。この物語は、ある君主が**恨み**のある身分の高い人物に刀で**斬りかかり**、傷つけたことからはじまります。君主がその人物に**貶め**られていたという事実にも**関わらず**、徳川幕府は君主に切腹を**申しつけ**ます。その君主のために、**配下**の武士たちが**浪人**となって**討ち入り**を**果たし**、君主の敵をとったという実話なのです。その後、配下の武士たちは全員切腹を命じられます。

　しかし、彼らは死の恐怖を乗り越えて、亡き主君のために働いたわけで、そうした彼らの行為は、まさに「忠義」を**全う**したとして、人々に語り伝えられたのです。

　「忠義」は、日本人があこがれる精神的な美学であるともいえましょう。

90

Loyalty

In the society of the samurai, the concept of *hōkō* ("service") was closely related to the concept of *chūgi* ("loyalty"). In other words, *chūgi* meant putting one's life on the line in service for one's lord.

Chūgi is at the root of everything to do with the samurai spirit; it is a basic value which requires the samurai to overcome the fear of death in order to maintain his loyalty to his lord.

It was expected that the samurai would do everything possible to maintain this virtue of loyalty, and that in order to do this he would constantly undertake spiritual, military, and scholarly training.

The term *hōkō* ("service") was used in a general way to refer to the service undertaken to repay *on* ("social debt"); in the case of the samurai, *chūgi* was at the ethical core of their *hōkō*.

There is a tale in Japan called *Chūshingura* with which all Japanese are familiar. Based on a true story, the tale begins with a certain lord pulling a sword at court and wounding a high official who had been maltreating him. Despite the fact that the lord had been responding to the bullying of the official, he is ordered to commit *seppuku* ("suicide") by Tokugawa shogunate. His retainers, who have become *rōnin* ("masterless samurai"), then carefully plan and execute the assassination of the official. For this, the *rōnin* themselves are ordered to commit *seppuku*.

This action on the part of the *rōnin*, overcoming their fear of certain death in order to revenge their deceased lord, has been passed down over the years as an example of what is precisely meant by *chūgi*.

Loyalty is a spiritual virtue highly prized by the Japanese.

□ 結びつける relate
□ 命をかけて putting one's life
□ 根本 foundation
□ 貫く uphold
□ 価値観 sense of values
□ 修養 self-improvement
□ 稽古 practice
□ 研鑽 diligent study
□ 核 core
□ 恨み resentment
□ 斬りかかる assault with a sword
□ 貶める bully
□ 〜にも関わらず despite
□ 申しつける order
□ 配下 subordinate
□ 浪人 masterless samurai
□ 討ち入り assassination
□ 全うする complete

孝
こう

「目上」、「目下」という年齢差に起因する人間関係の中で、最も大切なものは親子の関係でした。

封建時代、武士は親子の間でも厳しい「上下」の隔たりがあり、父親は常に一家の長として、家族を監督する立場にあったのです。

そして、子供は「目上」である両親に対して敬意を表し、常に大切に遇してゆくことが、儒教道徳の上からも強く求められていました。当時、武士の子供は、両親に対してあたかも身分の異なる人に接するように、言葉遣いも変えていました。

この親に対する心構えを「孝」または「孝行」といいます。

「孝行」の発想は、日本のみならず他の多くの国にも見られ、とくに儒教道徳の影響の強い韓国で受け継がれています。

現在、親子の関係は以前とは比べものにならないほど、カジュアルになりました。「孝」に基づいた行動様式は、今ではほとんどみられません。

しかし、「孝行」という概念はよい価値観として、今なお教育の現場などでも取り上げられているのです。

Filial Piety

Of all *me-ue* ("higher") and *me-shita* ("lower") relationships, the most important one is that between parent and child.

During the feudal period, there was a strict *jōge* ("hierarchy") maintained between parent and child, with the father at the top overseeing the entire family.

Under these Confucian morals, children were expected to respect their parents and always give them due consideration. At the time, children would speak to their parents as if they were persons of different rank.

This type of attitude towards one's parents was called *kō* or *kōkō* ("filial piety").

Filial piety is a concept that exists not just in Japan but in many other countries as well, including Korea, where the influence of Confucian morals is strong.

Compared to the past, the relationship today between parent and child has become much more casual. It is rare now to see actions being taken based on the principles of *kō*.

However, at schools and other places of learning, filial piety is still often used as an example of a strong social value that should continue to be respected.

□ 〜に起因する be caused by
□ 隔たり distance
□ 監督する oversee
□ 遇する treat
□ 儒教道徳 Confucian morals
□ 〜の上から on top of
□ 接する interact with
□ 〜のみならず not just 〜 but
□ 比べものにならないほど can't compare
□ ほとんど（ない） rare
□ 今なお still

93

しがらみ

　目上、目下、先輩、後輩、そして親子など、日本社会を彩る様々な縦の構造は、ある意味とても複雑で、それに対応するコミュニケーションスタイルも多岐にわたります。

　そんな複雑な人間関係を日本人は「しがらみ」と呼ぶのです。

　「しがらみ」とは、元々水の流れを止める設備のことを意味します。これが、複雑な人間関係を表現する言葉となったのは、人間関係が生んだ様々な「義理」に縛られて人間の自由な行動が束縛されるからに他なりません。

　したがって「しがらみ」という概念は、そのまま「義理」にも繋がり、そして社会での様々なモラルとも直結します。

　「義理」と「人情」の狭間で苦しむ人とは、まさにこの社会の「しがらみ」に捉えられて苦しむ人のことを意味しているわけです。

　日本人が、自らの人間関係のことを「しがらみ」と表現する背景には、長い歴史の中で培われた様々な常識や硬直した社会制度に、日本人そのものがとらわれていることを示していることになります。

　しかし、同時に、「しがらみ」は、人が自らの勝手で行動するのではなく、相手の立場や気持ちを考えてどのように動くかを判断させる、大切な価値観でもあるのです。

Barriers

Japan's vertical society, with its highly varied types of relationships such as superior, subordirate, senior, junior, and parent & child and so on is quite complicated, and requires one to constantly make choices as to communication style. The Japanese call these types of complicated relationships *shigarami*.

The word *shigarami* originally refers to a device used to stop the flow of water. The word took on its broader meaning in the sense that a person's freedom to act was restricted by the *giri* ("obligations") that he would incur.

In this way, the concept of *shigarami* is connected to the concept of *giri* and to other ethical and moral considerations in society.

It would certainly be the case that a person dealing with the difficult conflict between *giri* ("obligation") and *ninjō* ("personal feelings") would be an example of a person caught in the *shigarami* of society.

The use of the word *shigarami* to refer to the difficulty of relationships reflects the common practices of this inflexible society, which have developed over a long period of time.

However, at the same time it must be said that *shigarami* is a positive social value since it prevents people from acting for selfish reasons and instead encourages them to carefully consider the position of others.

□〜を彩る decorate
□縦の構造 vertical structure
□多岐にわたる wide-ranging
□元々 originally
□設備 equipment
□直結する directly connect to
□狭間 gap
□捉えられる be caught
□硬直した rigid
□社会制度 social system
□とらわれる be trapped in
□自らの勝手で for one's own convenience

8

神

かみ

The Gods

神
かみ

　日本人にとっての「神」とは、多くの場合、日本古来の宗教である神道での様々な「神」を意味します。

　神道は、明治時代に天皇を中心とした近代国家を建設しようとしたときに、国教化され、天皇の権威を象徴する宗教として政治的に利用されたために、大きな誤解を与えてきた宗教でもありました。

　神道は、元来ヒンズー教と同じ多神教で、日本各地に育まれてきた多彩な宗教でした。神道の信奉者は、滝や岩、そして湖や大木など自然の中に「神」が宿ると考えていました。日本人は農耕生活を営むにあたって、その地域を象徴する木や岩の精霊に豊作を願いました。そして村々の安全を願うための宗教行為の集大成でもあったのです。

　実際、石や自然物を崇めたり、水で清めたりする宗教行為は、北から南までアジア全般でみることができます。日本人にとって、そうした自然を象徴する事物の神秘を崇め、その前で身や心を清めることが、大切な宗教上の行為だったのです。神道は、こうした目的のために山にこもって修行し、鍛錬する山岳信仰などをも育みます。

　キリスト教や仏教などと違い、偶像を信仰の対象とせず、常に自然と向かい合うことが神道の特徴で、唯一例外として「神」の象徴として自然を映し出す「鏡」などが崇拝されることがあるのです。

　この古代から伝わる神道の考え方が、後年に大陸から伝来した仏教と重なり、日本人独特の精神的価値観が育まれます。

　仏教の修行の中に、神道的な身を清める発想が加わり、実際仏教の寺院に仏を崇める堂の横に、神道での「神」を祀る神社が置かれたりするのも、日本の宗教の特徴といえましょう。

　キリスト教とは違い、日本人にとっての「神」とは、人が自らの罪や贖罪を意識して対峙する「神」ではなく、自らを取り巻く自然への敬意と、清らかな自然に向かい、自らをも清めてゆく考えの中で創造されたパワーなのです。

The Gods

When Japanese refer to *kami*, they usually mean the gods of the Shintō religion, which has been in Japan since ancient times.

Due to the fact that Shintō was instituted as a state religion for political purposes at the time of the Meiji Reformation, using the prestige of the emperor as its symbolic head, this religion has sometimes been misunderstood.

At its roots, Shintō was a diffuse system of beliefs that developed over time in local areas throughout Japan and, like Hinduism, had multiple gods. The followers of Shintō believed that the power of these gods resided in waterfalls, rocks, lakes, large trees, and other objects of nature. As an agricultural society, the Japanese would pray for an abundant harvest to the spirits symbolized by these objects; these religious rites also became an opportunity to gather together to pray for the safety of these various villages.

From the north to the south throughout Asia, it is possible to find religions that worship rocks and other objects in nature and that perform purifying rites with water. For the Japanese, who worshipped the mystery symbolized by nature, purifying one's body and soul before these objects was an important religious rite. With this objective in mind, various types of ascetic training in the mountains developed.

Unlike Christianity or Buddhism, there is no worship of idols in Shintō, where the worshipper is always at one with nature; the only exception to this would be mirrors used to reflect the symbols of nature.

The native Shintō later mixed with elements of Buddhism from the Asian continent to create the unique spiritual values of the Japanese. This mixing of Shintō and Buddhist elements is a trait of religion in Japan, and can be seen in such things as Shintō-like purifying in Buddhist training; it is also not uncommon to find a Shintō shrine right next to a Buddhist hall of worship.

Unlike Christianity, where people are expected to atone to a god for their sins, the appeal of Shintō for the Japanese is to be found in the respect paid to nature and, through being unified with the purity of nature, to in turn become pure oneself.

□ 古来の ancient
□ 近代国家 modern nation
□ 国教化する establish as a state religion
□ 象徴する symbolize
□ 多彩な diverse
□ 信奉者 follower
□ 〜に神が宿る be inhabited by gods
□ 営む engage
□ 象徴する symbolize
□ 精霊 spirit
□ 豊作 abundant harvest
□ 集大成 grand sum
□ 崇める worship
□ 清める purify
□ 全般で overall
□ 〜にこもる stay holed up in
□ 偶像 idol
□ 〜と向かい合う face
□ 〜から伝来する come from
□ 祀る enshrine
□ 贖罪 atone
□ 対峙する confront
□ 取り巻く surround

禊 <ruby>禊<rt>みそぎ</rt></ruby>

35

　岩や大木など自然の造物に魂や神が宿るとする神道において、最も大切とされる行為が、そうした精霊に向かうにあたって身を清める行為です。

　この身を清める行為のことを「禊」といいます。特に、神道などで、神のそばに仕える者は、水などで身を清め、常に清潔にしておくことが求められました。

　この「禊」の行為が、その後様々な形で日本の伝統の中に残るようになります。たとえば、お祭りで体に水をかけたり、元旦に冷たい海に入って一年の無病息災を祈ったりといった行為が日本各地にみられます。さらに、今でも山岳信仰で、滝にあたって身を清める風習があることなど、例をあげればきりがありません。

　日本人は風呂が好きで、シャワーではなく、湯船につかる習慣があります。湯船につかった後で、改めて体を洗う風習は、こうした「禊」のしきたりにその原点があるのかもしれません。

　「禊」の行為は、単に体をきれいにして神に向かうだけではなく、行為を通して心の「穢れ」も清らかにしてゆくものと信じられています。

　昔の日本人にとって、日々の生活の中に区切りをつけて、心と体を清め、改めて神に向かう行為は、生きてゆく上での大切な「けじめ」でもありました。

　今も、神社にお参りをする前は、神社の入り口や前にある水場で手を洗い、口をゆすぎます。その後で、日本人は神に向かって商売や家庭の平安を祈願するのです。

神

Purification

The act of purifying oneself before rocks, trees, and other objects of nature where spirits and gods reside is considered to be very important.

Such an act of purification is called *misogi*. For those in particular who participate in the rites of Shintō, it is expected that they will purify themselves with water, always keeping themselves clean.

The act of *misogi* can be found in many different forms in the traditions of Japan. For example, throughout the country one can see people pouring water over themselves at various festivals; or one might see people jumping into cold ocean water on New Year's Day as they pray for good health in the coming year; or one might find people standing under a waterfall as part of spiritual training in the mountains. There are countless examples.

The Japanese preference for taking a bath instead of a shower—washing themselves outside the tub before getting in—may be related to this custom of *misogi*.

The act of *misogi* is not simply a matter of cleaning one's body; the Japanese also believe that this is a cleansing of the soul.

For the Japanese of old, it was important to mark the distinction between everyday life and the time one would spend before the gods by first properly purifying the body and soul. Even now, before entering a shrine to pray, one will wash one's hand and rinse out one's mouth. It is only after purifying himself that a Japanese will then pray to the gods for the welfare of his family or business.

□ 自然の造物 nature's creation
□ 〜とされる be considered to
□ 身を清める purify oneself
□ 〜のそばに仕える attend to someone
□ 元旦 New Year's Day
□ 無病息災 good health and longevity
□ 山岳信仰 mountain worship
□ きりがない countless
□ 湯船 bathtub
□ 〜につかる soak in
□ 改めて once again
□ 穢れ defilement
□ 区切りをつける mark the distinction
□ けじめ distinction
□ 水場 water place
□ ゆすぐ rinse out
□ 祈願する pray

穢れ（けが）

「禊」と深く関わる概念が「穢れ」です。

「穢れ」とは、**心身ともに**穢れた状態を示します。神の前に立つとき、人は穢れのない状態でなければならず、そのために「禊」を行うのです。

純潔という言葉があります。これは世界の多くの国にある古典的な価値観であり、**文化現象**ですが、**処女**であること、また子供のように純粋であることへの美学が神道における「穢れ」という発想の**対極**にもあるのです。

実際、神道では子供には大人にない**神的な**パワーがあると信じられており、**婚姻する**までの女性が純潔であることは、封建時代の道徳律などと**あいまって**、昔は大切なことであったのです。

子供のように**純真**ではなく、処女のように純潔ではない状態が穢れた状態とされ、人々は大人になってからも、神社などでそうした「穢れ」を**払おう**としたのです。

「穢れ」とは、単に**見た目**が汚いということを超えて、**邪悪な心**を持つことそのものを指す言葉として捉えられていたのです。

Defilement

A concept that is closely related to *misogi* ("purification") is *kegare* ("defilement").

Kegare refers to both the defilement of the body and the soul. One must be purified before standing in front of the gods in order to not present a defiled self.

Many countries have the traditional value of "purity" in their cultures. In Shintō, this concept of being pure in the way that a virgin girl or child is pure also exists.

In Shintō, it is believed that children have spiritual powers that adults do not, and traditionally, it was considered ethically important that a woman remain pure until her marriage.

For adults, who were no longer pure like children or virgins, they would try to rid themselves of their *kegare* at shrines or other places of worship.

Kegare was not simply a matter of being physically unclean; in looks; it also referred to the wickedness in a person's soul.

□心身ともに both the body and the soul
□純潔 purity
□文化現象 cultural phenomenon
□処女 virgin girl
□〜と対極にある antithetical to
□神的な divine
□婚姻する marry
□〜とあいまって combined with
□純真 innocence
□払う rid
□見た目 looks
□邪悪 wickedness

願
がん

　日本人は一般的に神社で神に自分の**実利的な**願いが**叶う**ようにお祈りをします。

　たとえば、子供が試験に合格して、高校や大学に進学できるように祈る人もいます。商売が**繁盛する**ようにとか、個々人によって様々な祈願をするのです。

　こうしたお願いを、真剣に行うことを「**願をかける**」といいます。「願」とは、「禊」を行って自らを清め、時には自分の**欲望**を抑えて心から「穢れ」をはらい、神に対してお願いをする行為です。

　たとえば、お酒の好きな人は、「願」をかけている間はお酒をやめるという行為で、自分のお酒への**欲求**を抑えたりするのが一般です。

　神道を強く**信奉し**、山を歩き、**滝にあたって自らを清める**行為を通して、修行を続ける人が昔から日本にはいました。彼らは仏教の影響も受け、**経を読み**ながら、「禊」を行い、心身を鍛えて**悟りをひらける**ようにと「願」をかけます。

　そうした人たちからみた場合、「願」とは単なる利益を得るために「神」に祈るという行為を超えた、精神的な高みを求めるための真剣な行為で、その行為を通してこそ**望みがかなえられる**という考え方なのです。

　そして、「願」をかけて神に祈る行為を日本人は「**祈願する**」といいます。祈願とは「祈り、そして願う」という意味の熟語です。

Request

It is common for the Japanese to pray to the gods at shrines for their wishes to come true.

For example, one might pray for a child to pass a test or get into a good high school or university; or one might pray for the prosperity of one's business. People pray for a variety of things.

When one wishes to make a particularly important request, the Japanese use the phrase *gan wo kakeru*. When making such a request, one will first purify oneself, ridding oneself of defilement and controlling one's desires, before praying to the gods.

For example, if a person is fond of alcohol, it is common for him to give it up while the request.

Since ancient times, fervent Japanese believers in Shintō purified themselves and strengthened their bodies and minds through walks in the mountains and standing under waterfalls and other training. Over time, these believers were also influenced by Buddhism, and in the Buddhist tradition, would read sutras and pray for enlightenment.

Gan is more than simply making requests of the gods; it is an attempt to improve one's spiritual being, and through that process, perhaps one's requests will be answered.

The Japanese also use the word *kigan* (literally, "pray request") when praying to the gods to answer requests.

□ 実利的な utilitarian

□ 叶う come true (wish)

□ 繁盛する prosper

□ 願をかける pray a god for a wish

□ 欲望 desire

□ 欲求 craving

□ 一般である common

□ 信奉する adhere to

□ 滝にあたる undergo waterfall meditation

□ 経 sutra

□ 悟りをひらく achieve enlightenment

□ 望みがかなえられる one's wishes will be fulfilled

大和魂
やまとだましい

　第二次世界大戦中、日本人を鼓舞するために盛んに語られた言葉が、この「大和魂」という言葉です。

　大和とは、古代の日本を示す言葉で、戦争中には軍国主義に利用され、この「大和魂」を強要された多くの若者が、戦いで命を落としてゆきました。

　元々、「大和魂」とは、神道に根ざした清らかさを根本に、自然と共にそこに宿る神々を大切にし、生活を整えてゆく精神を指す言葉でした。

　明治時代になり、神道が皇室の宗教として国家によって統率され、国粋主義と融合したとき、「大和魂」は日本人の強く優れた精神性を表現する言葉となり、以降この言葉は国家威信を強調するために使われるようになったのです。そして最終的には、「大和魂」に「忠義」や「滅私奉公」の価値観が集約され、日本が全体主義国家として戦争へと傾斜していったのも事実です。

　確かに、神道は日本独自の宗教です。しかし、そのルーツをたどれば、アジア各地に残る自然信仰や、ヨーロッパの森林信仰などにも結びつく、世界的に共有できる宗教でもあったわけです。「大和魂」はそんな神道を大切にする日本人の精神を表す言葉だったのです。

Japanese Spirit

During the Second World War, the phrase *yamato damashii* ("Japanese spirit") was often used to inspire the Japanese people.

Yamato is the ancient name of Japan. During the war, this phrase was abused by the militarists, and many young men were sent to their deaths in the name of *yamato damashii*.

Originally, *yamato damashii* was deeply rooted in Shintō, and referred to the spirit a person developed in purifying himself while being at one with the gods who resided in nature.

In the Meiji Era, Shintō became a state religion with the emperor at its head, and combined with nationalism, *yamato damashii* came to mean the strong national spirit of the Japanese. Thereafter the phrase was used to enhance national pride. And then later, in the 1930's, *yamato damashii* was combined with the concepts of *chūgi* ("loyalty") and *messhi hōkō* ("self sacrificing service"), as the nation slid down the slippery slope to a totalitarian state and war.

Shintō is in fact a religion unique to Japan. However, if one traces the roots of Shintō, one can find much in common with other animistic religions in the rest of Asia, that as well as in Europe. *Yamato damashii* is a phrase that expresses the importance Japanese place on the spirit of Shintō.

☐第二次世界大戦 the Second World War
☐鼓舞する inspire
☐盛んに often
☐軍国主義 militarism
☐命を落とす lose one's life
☐宿る inhabit
☐皇室 imperial family
☐統率する command
☐国粋主義 nationalism
☐以降 thereafter
☐国家威信 national pride
☐集約する combine
☐全体主義国家 totalitarian state
☐傾斜する lean towards
☐ルーツをたどる trace the roots
☐自然信仰 nature worship
☐森林信仰 forest worship

9

仏
ほとけ
Buddhism

仏
ほとけ

　日本に仏教が伝わってきたのは7世紀の頃ではないかといわれています。

　以後、仏教は時には権力者と結びつきました。後になると、権力者と結び権威となった仏教を批判する僧が出てきて、新しい信仰が生まれました。以来、仏教は民衆に広く伝搬してゆき、多様な形で受け入れられていったのです。

　「仏」という概念も、初期の仏教のように仏陀その人と深く結びついたイメージから、様々な宗派が発展してゆく過程で、より人の苦しみを救済する「神」のようなイメージに置き換えられていきました。

　また、それと共に、禅のように修行を通じて自らの中に「仏」を見いだすという内省的なものから、ひたすら念仏を唱え、そのことによって来世での救済を期待するというものまで、信仰の方法も多様に変化してきたのです。

　さらに、日本古来の神道とも融合して、共に信仰の対象となったのも日本の仏教の特徴といえそうです。

　神道には、来世に対するイメージが弱く、自然界に宿る様々な神を信仰し、そこからのご利益はむしろ現世に対するものでした。そんな日本人に来世観を与えたのが仏教なのです。

　もともとインドに生まれ、中国を通して日本に伝わってきた仏教ですが、現在我々が日本で目にする仏教のほとんどが、日本人独自の宗教観によって変化してきた、日本ならではの仏教となっている点は、興味深いことであるといえそうです。

Buddhism

It is said that Buddhism came to Japan in the seventh century.

At some point, Buddhism became tied to the power structure in Japan. Later there was criticism of that association from certain elements of the priesthood, and as a result of that, other sects came into being. Thereafter, over time, Buddhism was spread widely among the people, taking many forms.

While in its early period, Buddhism was more directly associated with the Buddha himself; in later times, as more sects developed, Buddhism was repositioned more closely in association with the "gods" as a belief to save people from their suffering.

Together with this development, Buddhism moved from being primarily a meditative discipline, such as *Zen*, in which one sought enlightenment, to a more diverse belief system, which also included many sects more centered on chanting as a way of finding salvation in the next world.

Buddhism also combined with the native religion of Japan, Shintō, to create Japan's unique form of Buddhism.

In Shintō, there is not a strong connection to an afterlife; rather, the belief is in the elements of nature and how those elements can benefit one in this life. It was Buddhism that encouraged a Japanese belief in the afterlife.

It is interesting to note that although Buddhism originated in India and came to Japan from China, the Buddhism we see in Japan today is primarily a product of the unique religious beliefs of the Japanese.

- □ 〜といわれている it is said that
- □ 権力者 a person with power
- □ 権威 authority
- □ 僧 Buddhist monk
- □ 以来 thereafter
- □ 伝搬する propagate
- □ 多様な形で受け入れる take many forms
- □ 仏陀 Buddha
- □ その人 oneself
- □ 宗派 sect
- □ 救済する save
- □ 禅 Zen (Buddhism)
- □ 仏を見いだす realize one's Buddha-nature
- □ 内省的な introspective
- □ ひたすら entirely
- □ 唱える chant
- □ 来世 next world
- □ 現世 this world
- □ 目にする see
- □ 宗教観 religious viewpoint

自力と他力

　禅のように、自らが行う修行を通して**信仰を深めて**ゆこうという考え方を「自力」といいます。

　それに対して、ただひたすら念仏を唱えることによって、来世での救済が約束されているというのが「他力」という考え方です。

　「他力」の発想は、より多くの人を救済しようとする**大乗仏教の流れ**によるものといわれています。

　特に**平安時代**には**阿弥陀信仰**が広まり、貧困や**病苦**、そして**戦乱に苦しむ民衆**へと受け入れられてゆきました。**念仏を唱えれば**、阿弥陀仏によって死後、極楽に迎えられるという考え方で、**この信仰を抱く人々の輪は**、16世紀には大衆運動へと発展し、**為政者をも脅かしてきた**のです。

　一方、禅宗のように「自力」を重んじる考え方は、武士などの**支配階級に拡大**してゆきます。

　このようにして、「自力」と「他力」という二つの発想は、日本の風土の中で、「自力」の禅と「他力」の浄土宗、あるいは浄土真宗として育っていったのです。

　現在でも「自力」、そして「他力」という言葉はよく用いられます。「人に頼らず、仕事は自力で**開拓しなければ**」といったように、宗教**とは離れた次元**で、こうした言葉が使用されているのです。

Self-power and Other-power

Seeking through self-discipline, as in *Zen*, to deepen one's beliefs is known as *jiriki* ("self-power").

In contrast to this, seeking one's salvation in the afterlife through chanting to the Amida Buddha is known as *tariki* ("other-power").

It is said that *tariki* came from the grass roots movement of Mahayana Buddhism to save more people.

Particularly during the Heian Period in Japan, the creed of Amida spread, as the common poor and sick and those affected by war found its message of salvation through chanting appealing. In the 16th century, the number of people embracing these beliefs grew to the point that they became a threat to the ruling class.

On the other hand, sects like *Zen*, with its emphasis on *jiriki*, became popular with the samurai ruling class.

In this way, the primary sects of Buddhism in Japan developed: the *Zen* of *jiriki* and the Jōdoshū and Jōdoshinshū of *tariki*.

Even now, the words *jiriki* and *tariki* are often used in conversation. For example: "Rather than asking someone else, one must do the work on one's own (*jiriki*)." In phrases like this, we can see how these words are used apart from their religious origins.

☐ 信仰を深める deepen one's beliefs
☐ 大乗仏教 Mahayana Buddhism
☐ 流れ movement
☐ 平安時代 Heian Period (794-1185)
☐ 阿弥陀信仰 the creed of Amida
☐ 病苦 pain of sickness
☐ 戦乱 maelstrom of war
☐ 民衆 common people
☐ 念仏を唱える chant the name of Amida
☐ 極楽 paradise
☐ この信仰を抱く embrace these beliefs
☐ 為政者 policymaker
☐ 脅かす threaten
☐ 支配階層 ruling class
☐ 拡大する become popular
☐ 風土 climate
☐ 開拓する develop
☐ 〜とは離れた次元で in a dimension apart from

あの世

　仏教での死後の世界、**すなわち来世**のことを、人々は**俗語**で「あの世」といいます。「因果」の項目でも解説しますが（第10章）、人はこの世での**行い**をよくすれば、「あの世」では極楽にゆくことができ、またよき人として**生まれ変わる**とされています。

　仏教が時代とともに日本で変化し、**哲学**としての仏教から信仰としての仏教へと変化する中で、この「あの世」の発想が大きく強調されてきました。

　それが、前項で紹介した「他力」の考え方と関係しながら、浄土宗、浄土真宗、そして日蓮宗といった新しい宗教運動へと発展し、**現代に至っている**のです。

　「あの世」**があるということ**は、人々が現世で苦しんだり失敗したりする**上で**の保証であり、救いであるといえましょう。そして、「あの世」があるということは、人に魂があり、死後も霊魂となってその人が存在することを意味します。

　それが、日本での葬儀やその後の死者を**弔う**様々な儀式へと発展していったのです。

　日本でよく語られる**怪談話**の特徴は、そうした霊魂が現世に対する恨みや**執着**が強く、「あの世」に旅立てず、幽霊となって現れるというテーマです。

　たとえば、**理不尽に殺された**人が、殺人者の前に恨みをもって**幽霊として現れ**るわけですが、その殺人者が処罰されたり、幽霊に悩まされて自殺したりした場合、幽霊となった霊魂は、安心して「あの世」に旅立ちます。

　そのことを俗語では「**成仏する**」というのです。すなわち、恨みや執着を**捨て**て、やっと「仏」の境地になって「あの世」、すなわち極楽に旅立ったというわけです。

The Other World

The world after death in Buddhism, or in other words, the afterlife, is called *ano yo* ("the other world") in colloquial speech. In the section on *inga* ("cause and effect") in Chapter 10, we will discuss how people who conduct themselves well in this world will go to paradise in "the other world" and then be reborn in favorable circumstances.

As Buddhism changed with the times in Japan and developed from a philosophy into a religion, this concept of "the other world" was emphasized more. As noted in the last section, this development was related to the concept of *tariki* and led to the founding of the Jōdoshū, Jōdoshinshū, and then later the Nichiren sects.

It may be said that the existence of "the other world" acts almost as an insurance policy for salvation for those who suffer or fail in this world. In "the other world," a person continues to exist as a spirit after his death in this world.

That spirit is honored in Japan in funerals and other ceremonies held after a person's death.

There are many ghost stories in Japan about spirits who continue to be bitter and obsessed with this world and are not able to go on to "the other world."

For example, a person who was murdered may go on to "the other world" only after the murderer has been executed or been haunted into committing suicide.

Going to "the other world" is called *jōbutsu* ("becoming a Buddha") in common speech. In other words, when a person is finally able to rid himself of the bitterness and obsessions of this world, then he is able to go to "the other world" of the Buddha, which is paradise.

□ すなわち in other words
□ 俗語 colloquial speech
□ 行いをよくする conduct oneself well
□ 生まれ変わる be reborn
□ 哲学 philosophy
□ 現代に至って down to the present day
□ 〜があるということ the belief in
□ 〜する上での for
□ 霊魂 spirit
□ 葬儀 funeral
□ 弔う mourn
□ 怪談話 ghost story
□ 執着 attachment
□ 理不尽に unreasoningly
□ 幽霊 ghost
□ 処罰する execute
□ 成仏する becoming a Buddha
□ 捨てる rid
□ やっと finally
□ 〜の境地になる reach the state of

もののあわ哀れ

42

仏教は、人の死を見つめる宗教でもあります。したがって、そこには儚い人生へのセンチメンタリズムが含まれています。

元来、仏教は、人や宇宙の移り行く姿を捉え、自らの欲望を抑えて自然な姿に心を戻してゆく自省的な宗教であり、哲学でした。

それが日本に伝来し、中世の矛盾の多い現世にあって、人々が来世に救いを求めるセンチメンタリズムへと変化してゆきました。

たとえば桜は、春、ほんの数日間花を咲かせ、あっという間に散ってしまいます。この移ろいの中に美学を見いだしたのが、「もののあわ哀れ」という美意識です。

人も、いつ死を迎えるか予想できません。特に昔は、子供でも大人でも、あっけなく「あの世」に旅立ちます。それは桜と同じように哀れなもので、人の儚い人生に「もののあわ哀れ」という美学を見出したのです。

平安時代以降、「もののあわ哀れ」という発想は文芸作品などに多くみられるようになりました。それが仏教での「他力」の発想と影響を与え合い、より宗教的な情緒へと変わっていったのです。

「もののあわ哀れ」は、日本人の美意識の奥にあって、現在でも多くの人が感じるセンチメンタリズムです。

人は儚い存在であるがゆえに、お互いにその悲しみを癒し合うことは、「情」の価値観にも通じるものといえましょう。

Pathos

In facing death and dealing with the fleetingness of life, an element of sentimentalism has developed in Japanese Buddhism.

In its origins, Buddhism was a religion and philosophy that dealt with the changing circumstances of humans and the universe, as people sought to return to their natural selves through self-reflection and the control of desires.

However, when Buddhism came to Japan and was faced with the conflicting realities of the middle ages, it evolved to meet the needs of those looking for salvation in the next world, and became more sentimental as it did so.

Cherry blossoms are one example. They bloom for only a few days in early spring before being blown off the trees. The sad beauty seen in this transition is what is meant by *mono no aware*.

No one knows when he will die. Particularly in the olden days, it was common to die suddenly at any age. As with the sad beauty of the brief life of the cherry blossoms, so it is with the *mono no aware* of the brief life of humans.

Starting in the Heian Period, one can see many examples of *mono no aware* in works of literature and art. The Buddhist concept of *tariki* ("other power") also came to influence *mono no aware*, giving it a more religious feeling.

Mono no aware is a form of sentimentalism deeply imbued in the Japanese sense of beauty.

It is necessary for people to support each other in overcoming the sadness of this fleeting life, and in that one will also find the concept of *jō* ("feelings").

□ 死を見つめる facing death
□ 儚い fleeting
□ 元来 in its origins
□ 移り行く changing
□ 自省的な self-reflective
□ ほんの only a few
□ あっという間に instantly
□ 移ろい transition
□ 見いだす find out
□ あっけなく easily
□ 文芸作品 works of literature and art
□ 情緒 sentiment
□ 美意識 sense of beauty
□ 〜であるがゆえに because of
□ 癒やし合う comfort each other

無常

43

「もののあわれ」が美学的な発想であるとするならば、それを仏教の視点からみた概念が「無常」という考え方です。

すべてのものは常に変化し、生まれた者は必ず死ぬ。そして栄華もいつか必ず衰退し、常に同じ状態を保つものはこの世にはないというのが、「無常」の考え方です。

ある意味で、これは仏教において仏陀が最初に抱いた悲しみであり、「無常」を感じることから、仏陀が涅槃にいたる足跡がはじまります。

日本では、そこに「もののあわれ」で示したセンチメンタリズムが付加されていったのです。

中世の叙事詩として有名な『平家物語』は、琵琶を奏でる法師によって全国に広められました。「諸行無常」という言葉が、その叙事詩の冒頭に語られています。これは「無常」という概念をより具体的に示した言葉で、この叙事詩では平家という12世紀後半に栄華を極めた一族が、ライバルの源氏に滅ぼされてゆく様子が語られています。「栄える者もかならず滅びる」と、叙事詩では語っているのです。

そして仏教の宗派の中には、「無常」であるが故に、阿弥陀仏を拝み、ひたすら念仏を唱えることで、苦しみのない来世へと迎えられると説く「他力」の宗派が生まれたのです。

Transience

If one considers *mono no aware* ("pathos") to be an aesthetic way of looking at things, then the Buddhist equivalent would be *mujō*.

All things are constantly changing, and all living things will eventually die. All that is glorious will decay, and there is nothing that will be able to maintain its current form—that is the concept of *mujō*.

In a certain sense, this was the first sorrow that Buddha embraced, and it was from this point that he began his journey towards Nirvana.

The sentimentalism of *mono no aware* ("pathos") was added to *mujō* when in Japan.

In the Middle Ages, the epic *The Tale of the Heike* was spread throughout Japan by monks who sang while playing the *biwa* ("Japanese lute"). At the beginning of the tale, it is stated that "everything is ephemeral, nothing is constant." This is a concrete example of *mujō*, as the story tells of the decline of the once all-powerful Heike at the hands of their chief rivals, the Genji. "The prosperous will always fall" is one of the themes of the story.

Then, in order to deal with the transience and pain of this life, sects centered around *tariki* ("other power") developed, using earnest chanting to the Amida Buddha to bring peace and salvation in the next life.

□ 視点 perspective
□ 栄華 prosperity
□ いつか必ず one day surely
□ 衰退する decay
□ 涅槃 Nirvana
□ 足跡がはじまる take a first step
□ 付加される be appended
□ 叙事詩 epic
□ 平家物語 The Tale of the Heike
□ 琵琶 Japanese lute
□ 奏でる play
□ 法師 Buddhist priest
□ 諸行無常 all things are impermanent
□ 冒頭 beginning
□ 後半 last half
□ 滅ぼされる be destroyed

悟り

　「諸行無常」を理解し、物事が起こり、変化する連鎖を見つめ、その連鎖の原因となる憎しみや欲望を絶つことによって、仏陀の境地へと至ることを「悟り」といいます。

　「他力」を唱える宗派では、ただひたすら念仏を唱えることで、阿弥陀仏が降りてきて人々を引き上げてくれると信じます。

　逆に、「自力」を唱える宗派では、様々な修行や瞑想を繰り返し、仏の心を体得しようと試みます。

　天台宗の本山である比叡山には、千日回峰行という荒行があります。行者は1000日にわたり比叡山や京都を毎日30キロから多いときは80キロ歩いて巡ります。そして700日目にある堂入りでは、堂の中で7日半飲まず食わず、眠らず、座らずの状態でお経を読み、毎晩谷底の水を汲んで堂内の不動明王に供えるという行をこなさなければなりません。

　こうして行を終えた人は大阿闍梨と呼ばれ、京都御所にも土足で参内できる特権を得ることができます。

　「悟り」を開くというのは、仏教徒にとっての共通の願いであこがれかもしれません。

　日本人の間にも、そのあこがれは静かに受け継がれ、今も多くの日本人の心の支えの一つとなっているようです。

Enlightenment

Having understood that "everything is ephemeral, nothing is constant," one then seeks enlightenment (*satori*). To do so, one rids oneself of one's enmities or desires by identifying their source and breaking the chain of such shortcomings, thereby advancing to the land of the Buddha.

Followers of the *tariki* sects believe that through earnest chanting they will be able to induce Buddha to come down and take them back to paradise.

On the other hand, the followers of the *jiriki* sects believe that through self-discipline and meditation they will be able to find salvation.

At the head temple of the Tendai sect, Hieizan, there is a rigorous regimen of training called *sennichi kaihōgyō* ("circling the mountains for one thousand days"). Over a thousand-day period, the supplicant walks between 30 and 80 kilometers a day around the Hieizan and Kyoto areas. Starting on the 700th day, there is a special period of seven-and-a-half-days during which the supplicant must read the sutras while not drinking, eating, sleeping, or sitting; each night he must also go down to the bottom of the valley to fetch water as an offering to the *Fudō Myōō*.

Those who complete this rigorous training are called *daiajari*, and as a reward, they are allowed to walk inside the Kyoto Imperial Palace with their shoes on.

For the followers of Buddhism, a desire to find *satori* ("enlightenment") is something they all have in common.

In Japan as well, the concept of *satori* has been quietly accepted and today is an important source of solace for many Japanese.

□ 連鎖 chain
□ 絶つ rid
□ 仏陀の境地 the state of Buddhahood
□ 降りてくる come down
□ 瞑想 meditation
□ 体得する master
□ 本山 head temple
□ 千日回峰行 the thousand-day mountain pilgrimage
□ 荒行 austere discipline
□ 行者 ascetic
□ 〜にわたる extend over
□ 堂入り the entry into the hall
□ 京都御所 Kyoto Imperial Palace
□ 土足で with one's shoes on
□ 参内する walk inside the Imperial Palace
□ 特権を得る gain a privilege
□ 心の支え spiritual support

禅（ぜん）

日本の「禅」は、海外で最も広く受け入れられた仏教の宗派の一つといえましょう。

鎌倉時代に中国から日本に伝わったとされる「禅」は、公案と呼ばれる師匠と弟子との問答を中心に修行をする臨済宗と、ひたすら座禅をする曹洞宗を中心に、全国に広がりました。

座禅という瞑想を繰り返しながら、自らを見つめ、そこに「仏」に通じる仏性を見いだそうとする「禅」の行為は、「仏」と対峙するというよりも、瞑想を通して自らと向き合う宗教として、日本では特に精神鍛錬を日課とした武士階級に支持されてきました。

「禅」は、日本文化にも様々な影響を与えてきました。

質素で簡潔な生活習慣をよしとする「禅」の考え方に基づいて造られる禅寺にはじまり、そこでの作庭術や、茶道のたしなみ、さらには武術や武士の生活規範に至るまで、「禅」の影響をみることができます。

ある意味で、今までみてきた日本人の価値観の中に、「禅」が見え隠れすることも否めません。たとえば、雄弁であるより寡黙であることをよしとする価値観や、自らの欲望を抑え、人に対応するコミュニケーションスタイルなども、「和」という日本人の基本的な価値観は、従来から日本にはあったにせよ、そこに「禅」の発想が加わることで、醸成されていったのではないでしょうか。

禅宗が支配階級の道徳律の背骨として浸透してゆくなかで、宗派の違いを乗り越えて、禅的な発想法を日本人が好んで、自らの生活規範の中に取り込んできたのです。

Zen

The Japanese sect of *Zen* is one of the most widely accepted forms of Buddhism in the West.

Imported from China during the Kamakura Era, *Zen* spread rapidly throughout Japan through the efforts of two sects: the Rinzai, which emphasized the question-and-answer approach between teacher and disciple known as *kōan;* and the Sōtō, which emphasized the meditative approach known as *zazen.*

Zazen's meditation places more weight on self-discovery than it does on intercourse with the Buddha, and in Japan this meditation became part of the daily routine of self-discipline and spiritual training for many in the samurai class.

Zen has also influenced Japanese culture in many different ways.

Starting with the temples themselves, which reflect *Zen's* emphasis on simplicity, the influence of *Zen* can be seen in such things as gardens, the tea ceremony, and the martial arts.

In a certain sense, it cannot be denied that *Zen* is present in some way in all of the Japanese values we have discussed to this point. For example, in the way that silence is valued over talking, or in the way that one's own desires should be controlled, or in the way that people communicate with each other—in all these ways we can see how the basic native value of *wa* ("harmony") was developed in tandem with *Zen.*

Zen permeated the ethical value system of the ruling classes, eventually transcending the sect to become an integral part of everyday life in Japan.

- 鎌倉時代 Kamakura Era (1185-1333)
- 公案 question for Zen meditation
- 仏性 Buddha nature
- 見いだす find out
- 対峙する face off against
- 自らと向き合う reflect on oneself
- 精神鍛錬 spiritual training
- 作庭術 art of gardening
- たしなみ etiquette
- 武術 martial arts
- 生活規範 code of living
- 見え隠れする be hidden in the background
- 雄弁 eloquence
- 寡黙 reticence
- 従来から heretofore
- 〜にせよ even if
- 醸成される be fostered
- 背骨 backbone

煩悩
ぼんのう

46

人間が持つ様々な欲望のことを仏教では「煩悩」と呼びます。

物欲、性欲、食欲、権勢欲など、煩悩には108種類あるといわれています。

除夜の鐘という儀式が日本にあります。大晦日に寺院が108回鐘を鳴らして、この「煩悩」を清めようとするのです。

仏教では、常にこうした「煩悩」をどのように克服し、「悟り」へと至るのかが課題となります。

仏陀自身、長い間瞑想を続ける中で、自らを苛む煩悩と戦い、最終的にそれを克服して「悟り」の境地、すなわち涅槃に至ったといわれています。

涅槃の状態を「寂静」と呼ぶように、それは「煩悩」によって心が騒ぐ状態を脱した、何もない静かな状態を指しています。

日本では、静けさを静寂という言葉で現しますが、それもこの「寂静」からきている熟語です。

日本人は「煩悩」という言葉をよく使い、「いやいや煩悩が多くてね」といえば、心配事や何かへの執着があって困っていることを示します。

そんなとき、日本人はふとお寺巡りをしに京都に行ったり、人によっては四国八十八箇所というお寺巡りの巡礼をしたりしながら、自分を見つめ直そうと試みるのです。

Worldly Desires

In Buddhism, the various desires that humans have are called *bonnō*.

It is said that there are 108 desires, including desire for wealth, sex, drink, power, and so on. In Japan there is a ceremony called *joya no kane* ("New Year's Eve bell") in which the temple bell is rung 108 times on the final night of the year in order to cleanse away the 108 desires.

In Buddhism, one must constantly overcome desire in one's attempt to reach enlightenment.

It is said that the Buddha himself meditated for a long period, battling with his own desires before finally overcoming them and finding enlightenment, or in other words, reaching Nirvana.

The state of Nirvana is called *jakujō*, and as its Chinese characters suggest, it means reaching a state of nothingness and quiet, having rid oneself of desires.

In Japanese, the word *seijaku*, which is an inversion of the characters for *jakujō*, is used to mean "tranquility" or "silence."

The Japanese often use the word *bonnō* in everyday conversation. They might say, for example, "I have so many desires (*bonnō*)." In this case, it means that they have worries or obsessions that are troubling them.

When faced with a situation like that, a Japanese will seek to right himself through self-reflection, perhaps worshipping at temples in Kyoto or making the rounds of the 88 temples in Shikoku.

□ 物欲 materialistic desire
□ 性欲 sexual desire
□ 食欲 appetite
□ 権勢欲 desire for power
□ 除夜の鐘 New Year's Eve bell
□ 大晦日 New Year's Eve
□ 課題となる pose a challenge
□ 苛む torment
□ 涅槃 Nirvana
□ 寂静 quiet and peaceful
□ 脱する be rid of
□ 静寂 quietness
□ 熟語 phrase
□ いやいや not at all
□ ふと casually
□ お寺巡り touring temples
□ 巡礼 pilgrimage
□ 自分を見つめ直す look at oneself again

くう
空

47

空気の項で、「空」という漢字の意味するところはすでに説明していますが、ここでは、仏教における「空」とはなにかを見つめたいと思います。

「空」とは、何もない状態、からっぽの状態を示します。「空」は、「虚空」という熟語によって、非常に小さな状態を示す言葉にもなります。それは、**自我**を限りなく小さくし、捨てることにより、自らの中に仏性を見いだそうとする仏教の根本的な考え方に通じる概念なのです。

「虚空」というきわめて小さい**単位**から、さらに**無限**に近く縮小してゆくと、そこに**涅槃寂静**という最小の単位に**到達**します。これは東洋での実際の数字の単位であると**同時**に、仏教でいう静かに悟った状態をも示します。

現代の**物質文明**では、生活を豊かにし、欲望を満たすことが肯定され、精神の自由は豊かさによって獲得できるものとされています。ここに記す「空」は、それとは全く逆を示し、欲望を深めれば深めるほど、**渇き**は増してゆくと説いています。

日本も**資本主義国**で、人々は金銭欲や物欲に体ごとつかっています。そして、確かに高度に発展した現代社会の中で、人々は精神的な疲れや渇きを抱いているのも事実でしょう。

そんな日本において、人々は心の奥底に、こうした「空」への**渇望**、そして美意識を今なお抱いています。

禅寺の簡素な庭を見るとき、どことなく安らぎを覚える日本人は数多くいるはずです。

Emptiness

In the section on *kūki* ("air"), we touched on the meaning of the Chinese character for *kū*. Here we will focus on the Buddhist implications of the character.

Kū denotes a state of nothingness, of being completely empty. In Japanese the word *kokū* also means a state of nothingness, but implies nothingness in a very small sense. One is able to find one's Buddha nature by shrinking down and ridding oneself of one's ego, the source of worldly desires.

Going beyond the already extremely small size of *kokū*, one continues to shrink one's ego ad infinitum until one reaches the nothingness of Nirvana (*nehanjakujō*). While this same word is used in East Asia as a unit of mathematical measurement, it also denotes the state of tranquility one reaches in enlightenment.

In today's materialistic society, people try to find spiritual freedom through an affluent life and the satisfaction of their desires. *Kū*, on the other hand, is the complete opposite of this: the more one seeks to meet one's desires, the less fulfilled one will feel.

Japan is a capitalist country, and many people are able to meet most of their materialistic desires. It is also true that in this highly economically developed country, many people are spiritually exhausted.

Deep in their hearts, many of these same people would strongly like to experience the fulfillment and beauty of *kū*.

There are still many Japanese who can feel completely at ease when they experience the simplicity of a *Zen* garden.

□虚空 the void
□自我 ego
□限りなく boundlessly
□単位 unit
□無限に ad infinitum
□涅槃寂静 nirvana quietude
□到達する reach
□同時に simultaneously
□物質文明 material civilization
□肯定する affirm
□渇き thirst
□資本主義国 capitalist country
□金銭欲 greed for money
□体ごとつかる be immersed in
□渇望 craving
□どことなく somehow
□安らぎを覚える feel at ease

無
<ruby>無<rt>む</rt></ruby>

48

「無」と「空」とは非常に似た概念です。

仏教では、**絶対的なものは存在せず、全てに原因と結果がある**と説きます。したがって原因がなければ結果はなく、欲望がなければ、悩みは存在しなくなります。そうした因果関係を超えて、**いっさい何も無い状態に自分をおくことが「悟り」である**以上、「無」という考え方は、仏教の根本を示す概念といえそうです。

この**哲学的なものの見方**は、実は日本人の行動様式にも大きな影響を与えてきました。

「無」に至る最初の入り口は、**相対的、客観的に物事をみる**ことです。

それは、自分からの発想のみではなく、相手が何を望んでいるかを知ることで、人と人との交わりから生まれる因果関係を理解することを意味します。

この発想は、「和」の原理を持つ日本人には受け入れやすいものでした。自らの欲求を抑え、相手の意図を尊重しようという行動原理と、「無」へのアプローチが日本人のコミュニケーションスタイルに相乗効果を生み出すのです。

これが、「遠慮」の価値観にも影響され、日本人独特の会話方法となりました。そして、これが自らのニーズをしっかりと伝えるべきとする欧米人との間の誤解を招くことも多いようです。

「無」とは、**どこにも中心がない状態**です。

すなわち、自分の欲求が中心ではなく、そこには必ず相手の望みという別の軸も存在しているわけです。

究極の「無」とは、そうした欲求自体のない静かな状態に自らをおくことで、人へも救いを与える**平安な状態が成立する**という理想とつながるのです。

Nothingness

Mu is very similar to the concept of *kū*.

In Buddhism, there are no absolutes, and all effects have causes. Because there is no effect if there is no cause, there are therefore no worries if there is no desire. Going beyond the relation of cause and effect to find enlightenment (*satori*) in nothingness (*mu*) is one of the basic concepts of Buddhism. This philosophy, this way of looking at things, has had a large influence on Japanese behavior.

The starting point for reaching *mu* is to look at things in a comparative and objective way. To do so, one must begin by taking the point of view of other people rather than one's own, and from there, one first understands the connection between cause and effect in human relations.

For the Japanese, who place such importance on *wa* ("harmony"), this is an easy concept to accept. In other words, the principle of controlling one's desires and respecting the intent of others meshes well with the concept of *mu* to achieve an effective communication style for the Japanese.

This is a conversation characteristic of the Japanese and reflects their sense of reserve (*enryo*). It seems that this reserved approach often leads to misunderstandings with Westerners, who tend to put their own needs first.

In the concept of *mu*, one has no center in oneself. In other words, the desires of others are always central, rather than one's own desires.

Taking oneself to the ultimate state of *mu* puts one in an ideal condition of tranquility, which in turn allows one to help others.

□ 絶対的なもの absolute

□ 原因 cause

□ 結果 effect

□ 因果関係 relation of cause and effect

□ いっさい completely

□ 哲学的なものの見方 philosophical view of things

□ 入り口 starting point

□ 相対的な comparative

□ 客観的な objective

□ 〜のみではなく not only ~ but

□ 人と人との交わり fellowship with people

□ 相乗効果 synergy

□ 誤解を招く lead to misunderstandings

□ どこにも中心がない状態 a state of no center anywhere

□ 軸 axis

□ 究極の ultimate

□ 平安な peaceful

□ 成立する be established

10

縁

えん

Relatonships

縁
えん

49

「縁」とは、人と人との出会いや離別からできる人間関係、そしてそこで培われるつながりを指す言葉です。

「縁」とは仏教で使われる言葉でもあり、仏によって結びつけられる人と人との関係を意味します。

「袖触れ合うも他生の縁」という言葉が日本にはあり、それは、ちょっとした出会いでも大切にしなければという意味を含んでいます。相手に敬意を払い、相手と最大限の「和」を保ってゆくことが、「縁」が求める理想です。

残念ながら、そうした考え方は、現代のビジネス文化の中では廃れつつあります。しかし、日本人が今なお、深い人間関係を求めようとしている傾向があることも事実です。ビジネスでも、お互いによく知り合うために食事やお酒を共にしたり、時にはプライベートな質問をしたりする背景には、こうした「縁」を大切にしようという伝統があるのです。

また、「縁」には人の力ではどうしようもない定めが作用していると仏教では教えます。

昔から、人に良くすれば、それは必ず自分の未来、また遠い将来生まれ変わった自分に返ってくるという発想があり、過去、あるいは前世の所行によって導かれる人との出会いや関係が「縁」という言葉で表されるのです。

「縁」は、人との関係を大切にしなければならないという、仏教によって生み出された倫理であり、道徳的な概念ともいえるのです。

Relationships

En describes the concept of a relationship, from first meeting to farewell, and the bond that is developed therein.

    En is also a word used in Buddhism, meaning the relationships that are created by the Buddha as he brings one person together with another.

    There is a phrase in Japanese that "even a chance encounter is preordained." This means that all relationships are important and must be taken good care of. The ideal is to treat each person with respect and make the utmost effort to maintain *wa* ("harmony").

    Unfortunately, in today's global business culture, there seems to be a trend towards treating relationships as less important. However, it is a fact that the Japanese continue to place a great deal of importance on relationships. Even in business, the tradition of *en* remains alive as people get to know each other better by eating and drinking together, and on occasion, asking personal questions as well.

    It is taught in Buddhism that one cannot change the *en* in one's life. This concept is called *sadame*.

    Since olden times in Japan, there is the belief that if a person treats others well, that that good will return to him in the future of this life or in a life yet to come. The relationships that a person has formed through one's acts in the past of this life or an earlier life are called *en*.

    En is a moral concept, grown out of Buddhist ethics, which emphasizes the importance of human relationships.

- ☐ 離別 separation
- ☐ 袖触れ合う their sleeves brush against each other
- ☐ 他生の縁 karmic bond from a past life
- ☐ ちょっとした trivial
- ☐ 〜つつある be in the process of
- ☐ 傾向 tendency
- ☐ 人の力 human power
- ☐ どうしようもない unavoidable
- ☐ 定め fate
- ☐ 作用する affect
- ☐ 人に良くする be good to people
- ☐ 所行 deeds
- ☐ 導かれる be guided

輪廻
りんね

　生きるものは全て宇宙の定め、そして「仏」の定めに従って、様々な生き物に生まれ変わり、生死を繰り返してゆくという考え方が「輪廻」の考え方です。

　仏教のふるさとであるインドなどでも、この考え方は古くから人々に影響を与えてきました。そして、「輪廻」という概念は仏教の伝来と共に、日本にも深く根をおろしたのです。

　「輪廻」とは過去から未来へとつながる生命の流れであり、来世でも幸福な人間として生を受けられるようにという、期待を人々の間に育みました。

　現在の日本では、この考えをそのまま信じている人はほとんどいないでしょう。

　しかし、日本人に来世観がなくなったかといえば、そうではありません。人は死後も魂となって、子孫のもとに現れ、時には子孫を守ってゆくものと漠然と期待する日本人は今でも多いはずです。

　また、現世で良い行いをすれば、それはどこかで必ず報われるはずだという期待は、今でも多くの日本人の心の奥底にあるはずです。

　日本に、死者を敬い、その魂を大切にしようとするためのお祭りや、仏教 行事が多くあるのも、こうした「輪廻」や仏縁という考え方と無関係ではないのです。

Reincarnation

In *rinne*, all living things follow the laws of the universe and the Buddha, being born into this world in one form, dying, and then being reborn in another form in a never-ending cycle.

In the home of Buddhism, India, this way of thinking has influenced people since ancient times. Later on Buddhism brought the concept of *rinne* to Japan, where it also became deeply rooted in the society.

Rinne is the transition of life that links the past with the future, giving each person the hope that he will be happy in his next life.

In present-day Japan, there may be few people who believe in *rinne* per se.

That said, it is not true that the Japanese do not believe in a future life. There are many Japanese who continue to hold a vague belief that one's spirit is present after death and that that spirit remains near one's descendants, protecting them at times.

Deep in the hearts of many Japanese is also the expectation that good deeds done in this life will be rewarded in a future life.

The concepts of *rinne* and *butsuen* ("Buddha's fate") can also be seen in festivals and Buddhist ceremonies where the dead are honored and their spirits treated with importance.

□生きるもの all living things
□ふるさと hometown or native place
□根をおろす take root
□生を受ける come into the world
□育む nurture
□そのまま per se
□もと nearby
□漠然と vaguely
□報われる be rewarded
□仏縁 karmic connection with Buddhism

因果

　「因果」はあらゆるものには原因があり、それによって結果が定められるという仏教の考え方です。

　そして、「因果」は、「**因果応報**」という熟語で頻繁に使われる概念です。

　輪廻の項目で説明したように、仏教には前世の**悪行**や**善行**によって人の**運命**が定められるという**運命論**があり、前世が原因であれば、現在の運命はその結果ということになり、それが「因果」という考え方となっているのです。

　「**因果応報**」とは、単に前世と現在との関係に**とどまらず**、一生の間でも、自らが**なした**事柄は必ず自分に返ってくるという教えに基づいた言葉です。たとえば、若い頃に**親不孝**をして、その後自分が親になったときに自らの子供に苦しめられることがあった**とすれば**、それは**典型的な**「因果応報」となります。

　また、**罪を犯して逃げられた**としても、後に**重い病にかかって苦しみ死んで**ゆくケースがあったとすれば、それも「因果応報」です。

　「因果応報」は、いま**自らを見舞っている災難**や苦しみには、必ずその原因が存在するという考え方なのです。

　原因と結果とを示す「因果」という考え方は、「仏縁」や「輪廻」という考え方とも関連し、「縁」という価値観を支える大切な概念となっているのです。

縁

Cause and Effect

Inga expresses the Buddhist belief that for every cause there is an effect.

Related to *inga* is the often used phrase of *inga ōhō* ("as a man sows, so shall he reap").

As we saw in the last chapter on *rinne* ("reincarnation"), the good or bad that a person does in a past life will determine his fate in his next life; in other words, the causes of the last life will result in the effects of the next. This is *inga*.

The phrase *inga ōhō* is not limited to the cause and effect of one's past life on the present; one's deeds in this life will also come back to affect one's fate in this life. For example, if one does not take proper care of one's parents, then one may not receive proper care from one's own children. This would be a classic case of *inga ōhō*.

Another case of *inga ōhō* would be someone committing a crime and escaping, but later becoming seriously ill and dying.

In the concept of *inga ōhō*, it is believed that there is always an earlier cause for the difficulties or pains that one may be suffering now.

It may be said that *inga* is closely related to the concepts of *butsuen* ("Buddha's fate") and *rinne* ("reincarnation"), and that it supports the broader social value of *en* ("relationship").

□ あらゆる every
□ 因果応報 retribution
□ 悪行 bad deed
□ 善行 good deed
□ 運命 fate
□ 運命論 fatalism
□ 〜にとどまらず not limited to
□ なす do
□ 親不孝 lack of filial piety
□ 〜とすれば if
□ 典型的な typical
□ 罪を犯す commit a crime
□ 重い病にかかる suffer from a serious illness
□ 自らを見舞う bring upon oneself
□ 災難 calamity

11

信
しん
Trust

信
_{しん}

「信」とは信ずることから生まれる固い絆や安定した関係を示す言葉です。

「信」という漢字を分解すれば、左の部分は「人」を意味し、右の部分は「言葉」を意味しています。すなわち、言葉によって約定された人と人との強い信頼関係が「信」となります。

信頼を築く方法は様々です。たとえばアメリカでは、信頼の証は、まっすぐに相手の目を見ることと固い握手でしょう。そうすることで、相手が何も隠さず、正直に話していると感じられるのです。

では日本での信頼の証はどうでしょうか。相手の目を強く見つめず、相手に配慮して婉曲にものをいい、時には本音をあえて喋らずに、「謙遜」して自らの望みや実力も誇示しないことが相手から信頼されるコツかもしれません。

こうしてみると、二つの異なった文化に生きる人同士では、同じ「信」の概念を大切にするにしても、その表現の仕方は正反対ということになります。これは、ある意味ではとても危険なことと言えましょう。

言葉さえ通じれば、人はみな同じという考え方がいかに深刻な誤解の原因になるかということは、この「信」という概念に対する行動様式の違いをみると明白です。

Trust

Shin refers to a strong and stable bond established between two or more people.

If one breaks down the Chinese character for *shin*, one will see that the left side means "person," while the right side means "speak." In other words, the speech exchanged between people become the promises which result in a strong relationship of trust.

Trust may be gained in different ways. For example, Americans try to gain trust by looking directly into the other person's eyes and making a strong handshake. By doing this, it is felt that one is making his thoughts clear, without hiding anything.

In Japan, on the other hand, it may be said that trust is gained by being modest and not putting one's desires first, by being sensitive to the other person's position and speaking in an indirect manner as necessary, and by not looking into the other person's eyes in too aggressive a manner.

In this way, we can see that while both cultures have their own way of expressing trust, they are in fact completely the opposite of each other. This can be a dangerous thing.

It is clear from this discussion about *shin* how serious misunderstandings can occur by assuming that people are the same simply if they can speak each other's language.

□固い絆 stable bond

□〜を分解する disassemble

□約定する agree

□信頼関係 relationship of trust

□〜を築く build

□固い握手 strong handshake

□〜に配慮する be thoughtful of

□婉曲に in an indirect manner

□本音 what one really thinks

□コツ knack

□正反対 completely the opposite

□ある意味では in a sense

□〜さえすれば as long as

141

仁
（じん）

　「仁」という漢字を分解すると、左側が「人」、右側が「二」で、人が二人という意味になります。人が二人になったとき、お互いのことを意識し、相手にどのように対応するか考えます。つまり、そこに社会というものが生まれるのです。

　「仁」とは、その人と人との接し方、社会での振る舞い方の**知恵**と愛情を示す言葉で、古代中国の**儒教**の**根本概念**を現す漢字として日本にも伝わりました。

　古代、**国を治める**には、社会においては「上」を敬い、「下」を慈しみ、家庭においては父母に「孝」を尽くし、隣人を大切にしてゆくような社会をつくることが必要とされました。「仁」は、そうした考えを示す言葉です。

　儒教は、日本に伝来して以来、支配階級の規律や**心得**の哲学として取り入れられ、日本人の道徳律に大きな影響を与えてきました。特に江戸時代にその影響は強く、儒教の一派である朱子学が**身分制度を維持する思想的背景**として取り入れられ、徳川幕府の基本理念となりました。

　「仁」をしっかりと**心得**、**実践する人**が「信」に足る、すなわち「信用」できる人として尊敬されたのです。

　儒教の**始祖**である孔子の言葉をまとめた論語に、「**巧言令色、鮮なし仁**」という有名な言葉があります。これは言葉が**巧み**で、**愛想のよい表情**をする人間ほど、思いやりや**慈しみの心**が少ないものだという意味の**格言**です。

　この言葉からも理解できるように、日本人が寡黙であることを美徳とする背景には、儒教の影響も強くあるのです。

Benevolence

If we break down the Chinese character for *jin*, we will see that the left side of *jin* is the character for "person," while the right side is the character for "two." When two people get together, each is aware of the other person and must consider how to deal with that person. In other words, this is where this phenomenon we call "society" begins.

The concept of *jin* came to Japan from China early on as one of the basic tenets of Confucianism, denoting this interaction between people as knowledge and love are exchanged.

In ancient times, in order to maintain stability throughout the country, those above oneself were respected, those below were cherished, in the home filial piety was observed with one's parents, and one took good care of one's neighbors. *Jin* reflects the values inherent in these actions.

After arriving in Japan, Confucianism became an important part of the moral code and philosophy of the ruling class, and subsequently came to have a large influence over the ethics of all Japanese. This influence was particularly strong during the Edo Period, when the teachings of the Shushi school of Confucianism were used to support the strict class system of the Tokugawa government.

Those who actually lived their lives in keeping with the practices of *jin* were respected as people who could be trusted.

There is a famous saying by Confucius: "The man of flowery speech knows little about benevolence." What this means is that the more skilled a person is in flowery speech, the less sincere he is in his heart about the needs and feelings of others.

These words reflect again the strong influence of Confucianism in the importance the Japanese ascribe to the virtue of taciturnity.

□知恵 knowledge
□儒教 Confucianism
□根本概念 basic tenet
□国を治める govern a country
□慈しむ cherish
□尽くす devote oneself
□心得 understanding
□〜の一派 a form of
□朱子学 Neo-Confucianism
□身分制度 class system
□維持する maintain
□思想的背景 ideological background
□心得る understand
□実践する practice
□〜に足る be worthy of
□始祖 founder
□孔子 Confucious
□論語 Analects
□巧言令色、鮮し仁 Fine words and an insinuating appearance are seldom associated with true virtue.
□巧み skilled
□愛想のよい amiable
□慈しみの心 kindness
□格言 proverb

仁義
じんぎ

　「仁」を実践するには、人と人との約束事、すなわち「義」を大切にしなければなりません。「義」とはすでに解説した「義理」に通じる考え方と思えばいいでしょう。

　この二つの漢字を合わせると「仁義」となり、人と人との約束事をしっかりと守ることの大切さを説く熟語となるのです。

　もちろん、「仁義」は武士などの支配階級では**「忠義」**という言葉に置き換えられ、大切な価値観として尊重されました。

　そして、**庶民レベル**では、友人との約束や、人から与えられた「恩」に対して**ありがたく思う**ことが、「仁義」と**解釈**されてきました。そういう意味で、「仁義」は、やくざの世界などでは特に重んじられ、親分と子分との間の「仁義」をめぐる葛藤などは、今でも**映画の題材**として取り上げられています。

　言い換えれば、「仁義」を守ることが「信」につながり、「信」を得るためには、「仁義」に厚い心を持つことが大切です。

　「内」と意識した人間へは、その人を裏切らないように、「仁義」がうまれます。相手に対して「仁義」を感じることが、相手への「情」にもつながるのです。

Moral Code

In order to be a person of benevolence (*jin*), one must honor one's *gi* ("commitments"). In this case, *gi* is the same Chinese character used in *giri* ("obligations"), which we discussed earlier, and the two words have the same basic meaning.

If we combine the characters for *jin* and *gi*, we get *jingi*, which, as we noted above, denotes the importance of honoring one's commitments.

Among the ruling classes, the word *chūgi* ("loyalty") could be substituted for *jingi*. *Chūgi* was of course a particularly important value for the ruling classes.

Among the common people, on the other hand, *jingi* was interpreted as the promises kept among friends or the *on* ("social debt") that had been incurred with someone. *Jingi* in this sense is an especially important value for the yakuza, and there are even now many movies made where the central theme is complications in the commitments between a yakuza boss and his underling.

Putting it another way, honoring one's moral code (*jingi*) engenders trust (*shin*), and in turn trust strengthens one's commitment to one's moral code.

In order to not betray those who are in one's inner circle (*uchi*), one must have *jingi*. Having a sense of *jingi* means that one also has a sense of affection (*jō*) for those with whom one interacts.

□義 honor or duty
□忠義 loyalty
□置き換える substitute
□庶民 common people
□ありがたく思う appreciate
□解釈する interpret
□やくざ Japanese Mafia
□映画の題材 subject of the film
□言い換えれば in other words
□厚い deep or profound

12

徳

とく

Virtue

徳
とく

55

「徳」とは、日本人の価値観に精通し、それを実践し、そのことによって世の中にも必要とされる知性を指します。

したがって、「徳」のある人とは、人から尊敬され、何か必要なことがあれば、その人の意見を求め、時にはその人に教えを請います。

では、「徳」のある人物とはどのような人物像でしょうか。

まず、なんといってもその人は「謙譲」の精神をもって、常に控えめで、自分をアピールすることなど決してありません。腰が低く、「情」と「義理」とをよく理解しています。

その人は、しかも「道」を極めた「匠」かもしれません。しかし、すでに世の中の酸いも甘いも知り尽くし、厳しさよりも、穏やかさをもって人を包み込むような人かもしれません。

「徳」のある人は、人生の達人で、決して堅物ではありません。礼儀作法をしっかりと嗜み、道徳をよく心得ながらも、楽しむことにかけても達人です。日本人の知恵や価値観を集約した知恵。それが「徳」の意味するところなのです。

Virtue

The principle of *toku* ("virtue") is known and practiced by the Japanese, and through *toku* one learns what is necessary to be wise.

People of virtue are respected, and when necessary, a person will seek out their opinion or ask that they serve as a teacher.

What type of a person would we describe as being virtuous?

First, such a person is *kenjō* ("modest"), never seeking to blindly promote his own interests. He also has a good understanding of *jō* ("feelings") and *giri* ("obligation").

Furthermore, such a person may have the *takumi* ("skill") to "take the road (*michi*) as far as it will go." But it is also true that such a person may have already reached a point where he is confident and settled, and is neither bitter nor naive about life.

A virtuous person has mastered life, and knows how to adjust to its twists and turns. He is also a master of being able to enjoy life, following proper etiquette with grace while maintaining an ethical spirit. Being able to integrate wisdom with principle—this is the definition of *toku*.

☐ 精通する master or excel at

☐ 知性 intelligence

☐ 教えを請う ask someone for instruction

☐ 人物像 public image

☐ なんといっても after all

☐ 決してありえない never

☐ 腰が低い humble

☐ 匠 artisan

☐ 酸いも甘いも知り尽くす taste the sweets and bitters of life

☐ 穏やかさ gentleness

☐ 人を包み込む embrace or envelop people

☐ 人生の達人 expert or guru of life

☐ 堅物 stiff person

☐ 嗜む enjoy or appreciate

☐ 集約した知恵 aggregated wisdom

56

「名」とは、人の表の顔です。元々「名」は人の名前のことで、その人にとって最も大切なアイデンティティとなります。

　そして「名」は、その人にとっての名誉、そして地位をも意味します。社会的にしっかりとした地位を築いたとき、人はあの人は「名を成した」といいます。そして一般的に「名」を成した人は、「徳」をも備えていることが期待されます。

　「名」を成すということは、出世し人々から尊敬される人のことですから、そのことによって、その人は、外見上は少なくとも名誉を勝ち得たことになります。そのような人にとって名誉を維持することはとても重要です。名誉とは、精神的に高潔であることと、社会的に認められことの二つの側面を持ちますが、時にはその二つは矛盾することもあります。武士にとっては、精神的に高潔であることが本当の名誉とされていたのですが、現実はというと、やはり人間は弱い者で、表面上の社会的地位を維持することによって、「名」を維持してきた人が多いようです。

　「名」を維持することが、もし、何らかの理由で困難になったとき、その名は「恥」で汚されることになります。

Name

Na ("name") is the outward representation of a person's face. The root meaning of *na* is "name," an essential aspect of a person's identity.

Na also refers to a person's honor and position. When a person has built a solid position for himself in society, that person is said to have "established a name" (*na wo nashita*). It is expected that such a person will be virtuous.

A person who has established his name (*na*) is respected by people, meaning that, at least for outward appearances, he has earned a certain degree of honor and prestige. For such a person, it is very important that he maintain his honor. There are two aspects to honor: the internal integrity that one maintains and the external recognition that comes from society. Sometimes these two aspects of honor can be in conflict with each other. For the samurai, internal integrity was supposed to be the true definition of honor, but being human, it seems that in many cases, the external recognition of society was just as important, if not more so.

Maintaining one's *na* becomes difficult if, for some reason, one stains one's name with *haji* ("shame").

□ 表の顔 public image
□ 名誉 honor
□ 名を成す establish one's name
□ 備える equip
□ 出世する rise in life
□ 外見上は outwardly
□ 少なくとも at least
□ 高潔 integrity
□ 側面 aspect
□ 現実はというと in real life
□ 何らかの理由で for some reason
□ 汚す stain

恥
はじ

57

「名」は「恥」と表裏一体の価値観です。

「恥」とは、単に恥ずかしいことではなく、自らが大切にする「名」を汚すことによって**損なわれる**名誉心を意味する言葉です。

欧米の人は、キリスト教的な倫理観にそぐわない行為をしたときに、「罪」の意識を感じるといわれています。それに対して日本人は、「罪」ではなく「恥」の意識を抱くわけです。

「恥」とは、内省的に自らに問いかけて恥ずかしく思う他に、**共同体の他の人々**に対して恥ずかしく思うという意識もついてきます。常に他とのバランスの中で、自らが特に**過ちなどを犯して特異な**状況になることに対して、人は「恥」の意識をもつのです。

たとえば、死を畏れて戦いから逃げてしまった武士がいるとして、その武士は自らの弱い心を見つめて**恥じ入る**のと同時に、家族や同僚や**同郷の人々**、そして自らが仕える君主に対して「恥」の念を持ちます。

また、儒教的な観点からは、先祖に対して恥ずかしく思うといったように、祖先、時には子孫への「恥」という**多面的な**意識を抱くのです。

確かに、「和」を重んずるせいか、日本人は自らが行動するとき、常に他人のことを気にする傾向にあります。他人と異なる行動をするとき、**多かれ少なかれ**日本人は「恥」の意識と戦わなければならず、それを克服して自らの**意思**を通してゆくための勇気が要求されるのです。

Shame

Haji ("shame") is the opposite side of *na* ("name").

Haji is not simply doing something embarrassing; it means staining one's name and thereby losing one's honor.

It is said that Westerners will view an act that is contrary to the ethics of their Christian moral law as a sin. Rather than sin, the Japanese are concerned with *haji* ("shame").

As well as an introspective questioning of oneself, the concept of *haji* also involves how one is viewed by the surrounding community. One must always maintain one's balance with others, seeking to avoid making a mistake that will put one at odds with the community and result in *haji*.

For example, if during a battle a soldier were to desert his unit out of fear, he would not only have to come to terms with himself about his shameful act, he would also have to deal with the *haji* he had brought on his family, his comrades, his country, and if he were a samurai, the lord he was serving.

As in Confucian thought, the concept of avoiding *haji* extends to one's grandparents and can also include one's grandchildren.

Most likely due to the importance placed on maintaining *wa* ("harmony"), the Japanese tend to always be concerned about what others will think. Whenever the Japanese do something different from what most other people would do, even if it is not significantly different, they must find the courage to battle and overcome their feelings of *haji*.

□〜と表裏一体 be inextricably linked to

□損なう damage or impair

□共同体 community

□過ちを犯す make a mistake

□特異な abnormal

□〜を畏れる be afraid of

□恥じ入る feel ashamed

□同郷 same province

□念 feeling

□多面的な many-sided

□〜を気にする worry about

□多かれ少なかれ be more or less

□意思を通す assert or insist on one's will

徳

よく中国人は**面子**を大切にするといいます。

　その人の立場を**尊重**し、その人の**体裁**を傷つけ**ないようにする**ことを、中国の人は「その人の面子を守る」といいます。

　日本にも面子の概念も「面目」という言葉も存在します。自らの名誉を大切にし、自らの名に恥じないよう**気をつかって**ゆくことを、人は「**面目を保つ**」というのです。

　日本人は、「**面目**」**が潰れた**とき、「**恥**」を意識し、「面目」が潰れる原因をつくった人に対して**怒り**を覚えます。

　たとえば、会議で上司が自分の意見を言ったとき、部下がそれに**反論する**と、上司は「面目」を潰されます。ですから、部下は上司の体裁を保つために、その場では強く反論せずに、後で別の「場」をもって上司に自らの考えを伝えるのです。

　そうした意味で、「面目」という価値観は、「和」や「場」、そして「間」などの概念とも深く関連しているのです。

　人前で自らの意見を表明することを悪いこととは思わない欧米の価値観と、この「**面目**」という価値観は**鋭く対立**します。日本人にとって、「面目」とは相手の立場を考え、相手に「**恥**」をかかさないように「**配慮**」することの大切さを教える価値観です。

　相手の気持ちになって物事を考えれば、自然と「面目」は保たれ、人との「和」が維持できるのです。

徳

Face

It is often said that the Chinese place a great deal of importance on "face."

In other words, the Chinese "save face" when a person's position is respected, and nothing is done which would harm that person's social standing.

The Japanese have a similar concept of "face" (*menboku* or *mentsu*). One must "protect one's face" (*menboku wo tamotsu*) by taking care of one's honor and ensuring that one's name is not stained with *haji* ("shame").

A Japanese person will feel shame if he loses face, and he will be angry with the person or people who have caused him such shame.

For example, if a person were to openly oppose his boss during a meeting, the boss would lose face. In order to avoid this, the subordinate in this case would seek a different *ba* ("place") to present his views to his boss.

In this sense, the concept of *menboku* is closely related to the concepts of *wa* ("harmony"), *ba* ("place"), and *ma* ("space").

The concept of *menboku* tends to conflict sharply with the norms of Westerners, for whom voicing one's opinion in front of others is not a bad thing. For the Japanese, on the other hand, it is important to always consider the position of others and ensure that no *haji* ("shame") is brought to them. If one keeps the feelings of others in mind, *menboku* ("face") will be saved without making any special efforts, and *wa* ("harmony") will be maintained.

□面子 face
□尊重する respect
□体裁 appearance
□〜ないようにする try not to
□気をつかう take care
□面目を保つ save face
□面目が潰れる lose face
□怒りを覚える feel offended
□反論する contradict
□そうした意味で in this sense
□人前で in front of others
□鋭く sharply
□対立する conflict
□恥をかかせる put somebody to shame

分
ぶん

59

「分」とは日本に古くからあるその人の立場にあった**言動**を期待する価値観です。昔は身分の低い者には身分に応じた「分」があり、たとえば身分の高い人の司る領域に口を挟み、意見をいうことはタブーでした。そうした行為は、「分をわきまえない行為」とされ、厳しく**追及**されたのです。

現在では「分」は、自らの社会的地位や会社での上下関係などの中に**織り込ま**れた価値観となっています。

新入社員は自らの「分」を守って、「**先輩**」に敬意を表し、上司の指示に黙って従いながら、仕事を学びます。学校でのクラブ活動では、**下級生は上級生**が活動する場所を掃除し、言葉遣いも丁寧にし、それぞれの立場での「分」に従った練習をすることが期待されます。

この「分」を**逸脱した**行動をした場合、相手の「**面目**」を**潰す**ことになるのです。

縦社会の典型のように思われるこの「分」という概念が、今なお日本人の心の中に生きていることには**驚か**されます。

全ての人は平等であると規定されている現代社会においての「分」という考え方。それは、お互いに**摩擦**なく相手を尊重して組織や社会の「**和**」を維持するための暗黙の**了解**とでもいえそうです。

Role

The principle of *bun* concerns the "role" that a person was expected to play based on his position in society. In the old days, it was taboo for a person of low rank to approach or talk to a person of high rank. This was known as *bun wo wakimaeru* ("understanding one's role"), and such practices were strictly enforced.

Today the principle of *bun* is still commonly found in the *jōge* ("hierarchy") relationships, which one maintains according to one's social position.

For a young person just joining a company, he will play his *bun* by respecting his *senpai* ("seniors") and obediently following their directions in learning his job. In clubs at school as well, it is expected that each person will play his *bun*, with the newer, more junior students using polite language towards the older, more senior students, while also doing chores such as cleaning up after them.

When a person does not properly play his *bun*, he may "do damage" to the "face" of another.

It is surprising that this concept of *bun*, which may be thought of as typical of a classical "vertical society," is still alive now in the hearts of Japanese.

In today's society, where all people are expected to be treated equally, it can be said that the implicit consent behind the concept of *bun* contributes to the overall *wa* ("harmony") maintained in companies and other organizations.

□言動 words and deeds
□司る preside over
□領域 area
□口を挟む interrupt
□わきまえない indiscreet
□追求する criticize
□織り込む incorporate
□新入社員 new employee
□先輩 senior
□下級生 underclassman
□上級生 upperclassman
□逸脱した deviant
□面目を潰す damage someone's honor
□縦社会 vertical society
□摩擦なく without friction
□暗黙の了解 implicit consent

阿吽の呼吸

　ここに記してきた日本人の価値観に支えられた様々なコミュニケーションスタイルを使いこなすことによって、相手に敢えてすべてを語らなくても意思疎通ができる状態を「阿吽の呼吸」といいます。

　たとえば、相手の立場を理解して、自らの「分」をわきまえれば、口に出して説明しなくても、その「場」での言動はコントロールできます。

　「和」の精神が理解でき、「型」を心得ていれば、敢えて人に対してその行為について詳細を質問する必要もありません。

　すなわち、こうしたプロトコルがわかっていれば、言葉を少なくしても、相手に意思や意図を伝えることができるのです。

　言葉を交わさなくても、即座に相手の意図が理解でき、その期待に合致した行動がとれる間柄、すなわち「阿吽の呼吸」の間柄こそ、「内」の関係であり、本音で話せる親しい関係といえましょう。

　ある研究によると、日本人は欧米の人に比べて、言葉の行間の意味を理解し、より簡単に文脈で意思疎通ができるということです。しかし、この発想は、日本人同士の価値観に基づいた交流を理解できない欧米の人にとっては誤解の原因となります。

Intuitive Communication

For the Japanese, who with their shared social values are able to use a variety of methods to communicate, getting one's point across with a limited amount of words is known as *aun no kokyū* (literally, "breathing in harmony").

For example, if one understands the position of the person one is dealing with, and one is able to properly play one's *bun* ("role"), then one will be able to control the flow of the conversation of that particular setting and it will not be necessary to use many words.

If one understands the spirit of *wa* ("harmony") and the *kata* ("form") of the moment, it will not be necessary to ask detailed questions about what is happening.

In other words, if this type of "protocol" is followed, a person will be able to express his intent with a minimum of words.

It is precisely this type of relationship, where one is able to have one's intent immediately understood by the other person without the use of words, which the Japanese would describe as *aun no kokyū*.

Studies done in the past show that, compared to Westerners, the Japanese are able to fill in meanings based on context more easily. This can lead to misunderstanding on the part of Westerners who are unfamiliar with this type of communication used between Japanese.

□記す record
□使いこなす use thoughtfully
□意思疎通 communication
□分をわきまえる act appropriately
□言葉を交わす exchange words
□即座に immediately
□意図 intent
□合致する correspond with
□間柄 relationship
□行間の意味 implication, nuance
□文脈 context

諦観
てい かん

61

「分」という価値観を思い出してください。

　昔から「分」は、身分や上下関係と深く関わった価値観として捉えられてきました。その発想で人間全体を一つのグループとして考えれば、その上にあるものとは神や仏、あるいは宇宙といった、**人知を超えた**存在であるということになります。

　人間は人間である以上、こうした**超越的な**存在に対しても「分」を持ちます。たとえば、人は死を**超越**できません。また、**未来を見通す**ことや、過去を変えることもできません。

　そんな人間の限界を人間の「分」として捉えることが、人間としての知恵をもった人、すなわち「徳」のある人ということになります。

　「諦観」とは、そのまま訳せば「あきらめ」ということになりますが、実際は、何が人間の「分」であるかを心得ることを意味し、その**限界を知る**ことを「諦観」と呼んでいるのです。

　従って、知恵ある人、「徳」のある人は、「諦観」を**併せ持っている**はずです。

　人が新たなことにチャレンジすることはよいことである**としながらも**、人の存在そのものの限界を理解することによって、より人にやさしく接するというのが「諦観」の持つ美学なのです。

　「礼」という価値を知ることによって、人の社会での知恵を抱き、「諦観」を抱くことによって、より大きな自然や宇宙、そして神や仏の存在に敬意を払うことが、「徳」を磨いた知恵者に求められる究極の条件であるといえるのです。

Resignation

Please recall our earlier discussion about the concept of *bun* ("role").

From ancient times, *bun* has been closely related to rank and *jōge* ("hierarchical") relationships. If we think of humans as one group, then in terms of *jōge*, the rank above humans would be a god or gods, space, or something else beyond human knowledge.

Humans also have a *bun* ("role") to play in relation to such a transcendent being. For example, humans cannot overcome death. Humans also cannot see the future or change the past.

People who understand these limits in a profound sense as the *bun* ("part") to be played by humans may be considered wise; in other words, they are persons of virtue (*toku*).

Taken literally, *teikan* means "resignation." However, what *teikan* truly means is the wisdom of understanding human limitations and discovering what one's *bun* ("role") should be within those limitations.

It follows that wise and virtuous people will also understand the true meaning of *teikan*.

While it is a good thing to challenge new objectives, one of the virtues of *teikan* is a tendency to treat other people better, which may come from understandings our limitations.

To be recognized as a polished person of virtue and wisdom, the ultimate requirement may be that through our understanding of *rei* ("etiquette") and *teikan* ("resignation"), we pay the proper respect to our gods.

□ 人知を超えた beyond human knowledge
□ 超越的な transcendental
□ 超越する transcend
□ 未来を見通す see the future
□ 限界を知る understand one's limitation
□ 従って therefore
□ 併せ持つ have both
□ 〜としながらも while
□ 存在そのもの existence itself

13

美
び
Beauty

日本の「美」とはどのようなものでしょうか。

日本の「美」を語る上で、**際立った四季**があることは重要です。日本は**温帯に位置**するため、春夏秋冬、それぞれの**季節感**が際立っています。季節ごとの**風物**や美術や工芸、さらには日本料理があり、その季節ならではの特徴が活かされているのです。

また、日本人は**季節**の移ろいに、仏教での「無常」を重ね、儚い人生をそこに**投影させて**きました。日本の**古典文学**では、このテーマが常に繰り返されています。

こうした季節感は、日本人を**観念的な**ものより、むしろビジュアル的な表現方法へと**駆り立て**ます。

近世の絵画を代表する浮世絵や、現代の漫画やアニメまで、その**原点**をたどれば、**四季折々**の風物をただ**写生する**のではなく、デフォルメして表現してきた伝統に**到達**します。

たとえば秋という季節感をいかにして表現するかは、山野の風物をそのまま描くより、紅葉を幾葉か組み合わせ、美しい線で描いた方がより**鮮明**に人々に**訴えかけ**ます。

こうしたデフォルメによるミニマリズムは、古くは禅寺の**石庭**にはじまり、線と色の組み合わせのみで表現する浮世絵や、文芸の世界では短い語句の中に自然や事物への思いを盛り込む俳句などにみられる、日本の芸術の特徴といえましょう。

Beauty

What exactly is beauty for the Japanese?

Among other things, it must be said that within the Japanese concept of beauty, the ebb and flow of the four seasons is very important. Geographically located in a temperate zone of the earth, Japan is a country where summer, fall, winter, and spring can all be experienced to their fullest. Each season has its own art, its own crafts, and certainly also its own food, each of which reflect the nuances of that particular time of the year.

For the Japanese, too, there is the Buddhist element of *mujō* ("transience"), which adds to the sense of impermanence seen in the changing of the seasons. This theme is a common one in classical Japanese literature.

The Japanese tend to express this sense of the seasons more visually than conceptually.

Rather than simply sketching the various elements of the four seasons as they appear directly to the eye, a tradition of expressing things in a more indirect manner has developed in modern wood block prints, manga, and anime.

For example, in depicting a fall scene, one may be able to make a deeper impact by drawing the fine lines of colorful leaves arranged in a pattern rather than a broader scene of mountains and fields.

It may be said that this type of indirect expression and the minimalism with which it is associated are particular features of Japanese art. Starting in ancient times with the gardens of *Zen* temples, these features can be seen in the lines and colors of wood block prints as well as in the abbreviated form of poetry known as *haiku*.

□ 際立った distinctive
□ 温帯 temperate zone
□ 位置する be located on
□ 季節感 seasonal prominence
□ 〜ごとの each
□ 風物 scenery and customs
□ 季節の移ろい passage of the seasons
□ 投影させる reflect
□ 古典文学 classical Japanese literature
□ 観念的な ideational
□ 駆り立てる urge on
□ 原点をたどる get back to the grass roots
□ 四季折々の seasonal
□ 写生する sketch
□ デフォルメする transform, modify
□ 幾 some
□ 鮮明に in a vivid way
□ 訴えかける make an appeal
□ 石庭 stone garden
□ 文芸 literary arts
□ 思いを盛り込む put some feeling into

わび

　色とりどりのきらびやかなものより、簡素でひなびたものの中に見いだす美しさを「わび」といいます。

　15世紀、「わび」は茶道などと共に語られるようになった美学で、それは茶器や茶室など目に見えるものだけではなく、無駄を排除し、質素なライフスタイルの中にやすらぎを見いだそうとする禅の発想とも融合して、人々の間に広がりました。

　たとえば、宝石をちりばめた器で美酒を飲むよりも、素焼きのお椀で清水を飲む方が、より味わいがあり、風雅であるというのが「わび」の考え方です。自然の中に自らをおいて、身の回りのものは最低限にし、季節の移ろいを肌で感じることに心の安らぎを得、同時に世の「無常」を思うことができるというのが「わび」の概念です。

　「わび」は、日本人が最も大切にする精神世界でもあり、物欲による贅沢ではなく、精神的な贅沢を求める上での理想であるともいえるのです。

The Beauty of the Simple

Wabi is the beauty found in the simple and desolate, as opposed to the beauty found in bright colors.

    Wabi was a concept that began to emerge as part of the tea ceremony in the 15th century. Over time it spread across Japan not simply in reference to the simplicity of the tea house or the tools of tea, but more broadly in connection with the *Zen* philosophy of meditation.

    For example, *wabi* would dictate that rather than drinking *sake* from a cup elaborately inlaid with jewels, it would be more refined to drink spring water from an unglazed bowl. *Wabi* might be felt, too, when one is alone, surrounded by nature, observing the changing of the seasons and also sensing the transience of this life.

    Wabi is a very important aspect of the Japanese value system, where the ideal is found not in the luxury of things, but rather in the luxury of the spirit.

☐ 色とりどりの very colorful
☐ きらびやかな sparkling
☐ ひなびた rustic
☐ 茶器 tea utensils
☐ 茶室 tearoom
☐ やすらぎ peace, tranquility
☐ ちりばめる inlay
☐ 素焼きの unglazed
☐ お椀 soup bowl
☐ 清水 clear (pure) water
☐ 味わい flavor, aroma
☐ 風雅である be refined
☐ 肌で感じる experience firsthand

さび

64

　「わび」と共に、時には対で語られるのが「さび」という概念です。「さび」とは、古くなり劣化したものの中に見いだす美の世界です。

　たとえば、古い日本家屋の廊下などは、時とともに磨かれ風化して木目が見えてきます。そんな家に住めば、夜、雨戸がガタガタと鳴ることによって、冬の前触れである木枯らしを実感し、その音をじっくり味わいながら俳句をつくるといったことが、「さび」であり、「わび、さび」と一つにして語られる美学なのです。

　また、日本の仏像は塗料がはげ落ちても、そのままにされ、現れた古木の美しさの中で微笑む仏像に人々は祈りを捧げます。朽ちてゆくものへの美意識がなければ、造られた当時の彩色を施し、新しく生まれ変わった仏像を安置するはずです。

　実は、質素で古いものをうまく使いこなし、そこから茶道や華道といった様式美が生みだされたことからも理解できるように、「わび」や「さび」の世界はそれを「美」の世界へと高めた洗練なのです。

　日本庭園では、よく苔が使われます。

　石を配置するとき、苔むした石を置くことで、「さび」の世界を表現しようとするのです。枯山水という庭園では、あえて池を造らず、石と砂と樹木で自然を表現し、石庭では樹木すらおかずに石と砂のみで自然界を表します。

　それは簡素で古くなったもの、つまり「わび、さび」の概念で造られるミニマリズムの世界なのです。

The Beauty of the Decaying

The concept of *sabi* is often spoken of together with the concept of *wabi*. *Sabi* is the beauty found in that which is old and decaying.

For example, one might see *sabi* in the worn grain of the polished wood of the corridors of an old Japanese house. And if one were to live in such a house, one might experience *sabi* (or both *wabi* and *sabi*) in hearing the sound of the night shutters being opened or closed, and hearing those sounds, one might recall the cold of the winter and be moved to write a *haiku* poem.

In Japan, people may be seen praying to old statues of the Buddha where the lacquer has fallen off and only the bare wood remains. If there were no such appreciation of the beauty of the decaying, then these old statues would be repainted and restored to their original state.

As can be seen in the tea ceremony and flower arrangement, *wabi* and *sabi* are not only the appreciation of the simple or the old; they also represent the refinement of such elements into the realm of "beauty."

Moss is commonly used in Japanese gardens.

Sabi is expressed by using moss-covered rocks in the garden. In the style of garden known as *karesansui*, no water is used, and nature is represented only with rocks, sand, and plants; in the style known as *sekitei*, only rocks and sand are used.

This is a minimalist world created with the simple and the old, or in other words, with *wabi* and *sabi*.

☐ 対で in a pair
☐ 劣化する deteriorate
☐ 家屋 house
☐ 廊下 corridor
☐ 木目 wood grain
☐ 雨戸 night shutter
☐ 前触れ a sign
☐ 木枯らし a wintry wind
☐ じっくり carefully
☐ 塗料 coating
☐ はげ落ちる peel off
☐ 朽ちる rot
☐ 彩色を施す color
☐ 安置する place
☐ 様式美 formal beauty
☐ 洗練 refinement
☐ 日本庭園 Japanese garden
☐ 苔 moss
☐ 苔むした mossy
☐ 枯山水 dry garden style

艶とは、洗練されていることを示す言葉です。

「わび、さび」の概念からもわかるように、決して贅沢なものを着こなし、きらびやかなものの中に身を置くことが洗練ではありません。歴史的にみるならば、「わび、さび」は都会人の嗜みでした。こうした一見贅沢に見えないおしゃれな感覚は、そのまま時代とともに受け継がれ、庶民の美意識の中にも浸透していったのです。

江戸時代に、都会ならではの遊女との享楽や色恋が浮世絵や当時の出版物で流布するようになると、おしゃれに遊ぶことが艶なことだとされ、町人の間で、様々なライフスタイルが流行します。

特に、当時の為政者が質素倹約を法制化したこともあり、贅沢には様々な規制が押し付けられました。そうした中で、表には現れない贅沢さ、そしておしゃれが追求されたのです。元来派手好きな町人は、敢えて目に見えないところや、ちょっとしたアクセントに気を配り、贅沢を追求したのです。

艶とは、「わび、さび」の概念を取り入れながらも、派手好きな町人の生命力が融合し、都会的な洗練へと進化した美意識であるといえましょう。

江戸時代、「艶」のある人といえば、セクシーでおしゃれな人という意味で、庶民のあこがれとなっていたのです。

Refinement

The word *tsuya* means "refinement."

As was seen in our discussion of *wabi* and *sabi*, it is not considered refined to dress oneself up in luxurious and glittering clothing. From an historical point of view, we can see how *wabi* and *sabi* came to reflect the tastes of city people. Over time, this "non-luxurious" stylishness came to be a part of the sense of beauty held by the common people.

During the Edo era, what was *tsuya* ("refined") came to be influenced by what was going on in the licensed districts. Wood block prints (*ukiyoe*) of dandies with the women of these districts became popular, setting the tone for fashion and other aspects of the daily life of the townspeople.

At that time, the authorities had regulations in place to enforce a frugal lifestyle, and there were many restrictions on any ostentatious displays of wealth. Given these circumstances, the townspeople were forced to adopt more subtle expressions of luxury and fashion, using an accent here or there in their attire, or even in their under-clothing, which could not be seen.

It may be said that *tsuya* combined the concepts of *wabi* and *sabi* with the townspeople's innate love of the flashy to produce the big-city sense of beauty.

During the Edo era, a person who was refined was seen as someone who was fashionable and sexy.

☐ 着こなす dress up
☐ きらびやかな sparkling
☐ 〜に身を置く be in
☐ 歴史的にみる view historically
☐ 嗜み manners
☐ おしゃれな fashionable
☐ 遊女 courtesan
☐ 享楽 indulgence
☐ 色恋 romance
☐ 流布する circulate
☐ 質素倹約 frugality, thriftiness
☐ 法制化する enact
☐ 押し付ける impose
☐ 表には現れない be hidden
☐ 派手 flashy

171

雅
みやび

　京都は長い間日本の首都として、宮廷がおかれていました。

　その千年の歴史の中で培われてきた宮廷文化が醸し出す、優雅で洗練された雰囲気を「雅」といいます。

　宮廷やそこに生きる貴族によって守られてきた「雅」な文化は、浮世絵などに代表される町人文化が醸し出す「艶」と対照的な美意識です。

　15世紀後半から16世紀にかけて、日本は戦国時代となり、当時京都にあった幕府が衰退し、日本全国で大名という有力者が覇権を競い戦い合っていました。大名は自らの領国を豊かにするために、進んで京都の文化を取り入れます。その過程の中で「雅」が全国に広がっていったのです。

　17世紀に、江戸（現在の東京）が日本の行政の中心になった後も、朝廷は京都にありました。江戸や大阪は当時の経済の中心として、躍動的な町人文化が栄え、それに押されるように京都の文化は衰退してゆきました。

　しかし、「雅」という美意識はその後も受け継がれ、今では古都京都の美しさそのものを指すようにもなったのです。

　そして、戦国時代以来、各地に広がった染物や陶磁器などの工芸に代表される京都の文化は、今なおそれぞれの地域で保存され、多くの人が地方に根付いた「雅」な伝統を守っているのです。

Elegance

As the capital of Japan, Kyoto was the location for the imperial court for a very long time.

Over that thousand-year history, the culture of the imperial court developed a graceful elegance which in Japanese is called *miyabi*.

The culture of *miyabi* developed by the nobles at the imperial court was in direct contrast to the culture of *tsuya* of the common people represented in wood block prints (*ukiyoe*).

During the latter half of the 15th century and into the 16th century, Japan went through a period of almost constant war. During that time, the central government in Kyoto went into decline, as the *daimyō* ("regional lords") came to dominate the politics of the country. In their quest for power, the *daimyō* sought also to bring into their own domains the culture of Kyoto, and it was through this process that *miyabi* spread throughout Japan.

Even after the central government moved to Edo (present day Tokyo) in the early 17th century, the imperial court remained in Kyoto. During this period, Edo and Osaka became the economic centers of Japan and the culture of the townspeople flourished, while that of Kyoto faded.

The sense of beauty found in *miyabi* did not disappear, however, and even now when one hears the word *miyabi* one thinks of the elegance of the culture of old Kyoto. After the wars of the 15th and 16th centuries, dyeing and pottery and other handicrafts of Kyoto spread throughout the country, and today they continue to be strongly rooted in the local communities.

□ 醸し出す produce
□ 対照的な contrastive
□ 戦国時代 Warring States era
□ 幕府 shogunate
□ 衰退する decline
□ 有力者 powerful figure
□ 覇権を競う vie for supremacy
□ 領国 fief
□ 進んで voluntarily
□ 行政 governance
□ 中心になる be central
□ 朝廷 imperial court
□ 躍動的な vibrant
□ 押されるように being pushed back
□ 古都 former capital
□ 染物 dyed goods
□ 陶磁器 ceramics

色
いろ

67

儒教道徳の影響を強く受けた武士を除けば、日本人は一般的に性に対して開放的でした。「色」とは、絵の具の「色」という意味の他に、恋や性を示す言葉として、今なお使われています。

色恋沙汰といえばセックススキャンダルのことですが、江戸時代も、庶民は色恋沙汰が大好きで、それが当時の歌舞伎や文楽といった芸能の題材になり、浮世絵でも取り上げられました。

当時の幕府は、そうしたテーマを扱うことを規制しますが、人々はその網の目をかいくぐって逞しく創作活動を続けたのです。

「色」は「艶」にも通じ、都会人のお洒落なライススタイルとして支持された概念です。

たとえば、春画と呼ばれる浮世絵があります。これは、江戸時代のポルノといってもよく、男女の交わりの様子が克明に描かれたもので、今では貴重な絵画として日本のみならず、世界で高価な値段がつけられています。

江戸時代、庶民は奔放に「色」の世界を楽しんでいたのでしょう。

そして今でも、日本を訪れた外国の人は、日本の開けっぴろげな風俗産業の隆盛ぶりにびっくりするそうです。

実際、性に対するタブーの多いキリスト教やイスラム教の影響の少ない日本では、「色」という概念はそのまま人々に受け入れられ、性のテーマは漫画などでも頻繁に取り上げられています。

「色」は、日本人の美意識の一部として認知されているのです。

Erotic

Excluding the prudish Confucian attitudes of the samurai, the Japanese have in general tended to be open-minded about sex. In Japanese, *iro* refers not only to color but can also refer to love or sex.

The Japanese of the Edo era also liked their sex scandals, and these scandals were often used as the subject matter for the *kabuki* or *bunraku* (puppet) dramas.

The government at the time had regulations in place to restrict dramas using such themes, but loopholes were found and the production of these dramas continued to flourish.

Iro can also be seen as an element of being refined (*tsuya*), as part of the drinking and night-life culture of the big city.

For example, there are wood block prints (*ukiyoe*) known as *shunga*. These prints, essentially the pornography of the Edo era, today fetch high prices on world markets as precious examples of a unique form of Japanese art.

It seems that the common people enjoyed the world of *iro* without restraint during the Edo era.

When non-Japanese visit Japan, it seems that they are often surprised at the openness and prosperity of the country's "pleasure" industry.

Japan has little of the influence of Christianity or Islam and their taboos on subjects related to sex. Being more open-minded, it is common in Japan to take up themes related to sex in *manga* or other popular forms of entertainment.

For the Japanese, *iro* is seen as one aspect of their overall sense of beauty.

☐ 開放的 open-minded

☐ 色恋沙汰 romance or sexual affair

☐ 芸能 entertainment

☐ 網の目をかいくぐる slip through the dragnet

☐ 創作活動 creative activity

☐ 春画 erotic or pornographic woodblock prints

☐ 交わり intercourse

☐ 克明に in detail

☐ 奔放に freely

☐ 開けっぴろげな openly

☐ 風俗産業 sex industry

☐ 隆盛 flourishing

☐ 〜ぶり The suffix "~buri" describes how something is or does or feels

粋
（いき）

68

粋とは、「色」や「艶」の世界を心得えて、人生を生きる人を表す言葉です。

これはある意味で、江戸時代にあった都会的なダンディズムといえましょう。また、気の利いた気配りや、為政者の庶民の気持ちを理解した判断なども「粋」という言葉で表現されます。

たとえば、母親の病気の薬を買うお金ほしさに盗賊の盗みの手伝いをした者がいたとして、江戸時代に司法長官であった町奉行がその者の罪を許して仕事を与えたとします。庶民はそれを「粋」なはからいといって喝采するのです。

「粋」とは、小さなことでありながら、センスがよくアクセントの利いたことを示します。この事例の場合、町奉行が法制度を変革しようとすることは職務であって「粋」なことではありません。この各論でのかわいそうな犯人を救った小さな判断が「粋」なのです。

同じように、たとえば部屋の中の小さな花瓶に椿をひと折り入れておいたとしましょう。それは大きな花の飾り付けではありませんが、訪れる人にちょっとした安らぎと季節感を与えます。それが「粋」なアレンジなのです。

「粋」なことは決して雄弁であってはなりません。それはささやかで、目にはつくものの、普段なら気づかないようなことにちょっとした工夫や心遣いが施されているものが「粋」なのです。

Chic

A person who is *iki* understands the worlds of *iro* and *tsuya*.

It may be said that *iki* represents the "dandyism" of the Edo era. *Iki* can also be expressed in the thoughtfulness of one person towards another, for example in how people in authority might understand the needs of the common people in making judgments.

Let's say that in the Edo era, a person helped out with a robbery in order to buy medicine for his sick mother, and the judge, rather than sending the guilty person to prison, arranged a job for him. This would be applauded by the common people as an act of *iki*.

While an act of *iki* is usually small in scale, it has good sense and a strong impact. In the example used here, the judge is not trying to bring about a major change in the law; he is simply trying to help one unfortunate person, and that is why this is a case of *iki*.

In the same way, let's say that we displayed a single camellia in a small vase. Even though this is a small display of a single flower, it gives people coming into the room a sense of peace, while also signaling the season. This would be an example of an *iki* arrangement.

When being *iki* it is not necessary to be eloquent. One can be *iki* by doing a small thing to bring attention to something that would usually not be noticed.

□ 気の利いた thoughtful
□ 気配り consideration
□ お金ほしさに for money
□ 盗賊 bandit
□ 司法長官 attorney general
□ 町奉行 town magistrate
□ はからい arrangement
□ 喝采する applaud
□ 変革する transform
□ 職務 duties
□ 各論 specific case
□ 花瓶 vase
□ 椿 camellia
□ ひと折り a single branch with flowers
□ 飾り付け decoration
□ ささやか small
□ 工夫 contrivance
□ 心遣い consideration
□ 施す apply

幽玄
ゆうげん

69

「わび」や「さび」の概念で、飾り気の無い素朴なものや、古く朽ちたものをじっと鑑賞していると、そこに時を超えた不思議な奥深さを感じることがあります。その情緒を人々は「幽玄」と呼んでいるのです。

また、日のかげりや夕暮れ時に漂う不安定な闇など、自然界の微妙な移ろいの向こうに感じる宇宙の深淵にもつながる静寂も「幽玄」の意味するところです。

深遠なる静寂はまた「妖」なる世界でもあります。というのも、「わび」や「さび」は、永遠の時の流れの中で風化し、朽ちてゆくものへの愛着を語る言葉であり、それは「無常」の概念に従って、死にゆくことへの美学にもつながっているからです。

中世以降日本人に親しまれてきた伝統芸能である「能」は、まさにこうした美しさを追求した舞踏劇で、その多くに死者の霊魂が語る場面がもうけられています。

「幽玄」とは、日本人の抱く美意識の中でも、最も伝統的で洗練された美しさへの価値観であるといえましょう。

Profound Tranquility

As discussed in the sections on *wabi* and *sabi*, when one closely observes the old and decaying or that which is of extreme simplicity, one can be moved beyond time to feel a surprising profundity. This is called *yūgen*.

Yūgen may also be found in the uneasiness felt at the end of the day as darkness approaches, or in the subtle changes of the natural world as one looks into the tranquility and the abyss of space.

A profound tranquility is also part of the world of the bewitched (*yō*). In this same way, *wabi* and *sabi* are also connected to the aesthetic of death, as these sensibilities reflect the eternal passage of time and with it, decay and decline and the eventual transience to death.

The traditional Noh drama, a part of Japanese culture since the Middle Ages, places importance on this particular sense of beauty, often including scenes where the spirits of the dead speak of their trials.

It may be said that *yūgen* is a very traditional and refined aspect of the Japanese sense of beauty.

□飾り気の無い unadorned
□素朴なもの simple
□朽ちた decaying
□鑑賞する appreciate
□時を超えた beyond time
□奥深さ profundity
□情緒 emotion
□かげり declining
□深淵 abyss
□妖 bewitching
□風化する weather and decay
□能 Noh drama
□追求した pursued
□舞踏劇 dance drama
□もうける set up
□洗練された refined

風流
（ふうりゅう）

　月見というイベントがあります。中秋の名月とは、澄んでひんやりとした秋の空気の中にみる満月の美しさを指す言葉で、そんな月を愛でることを月見というのです。こうした伝統的な美意識を体験することを、日本人は「風流」と表現します。

　この章に記した日本人の美意識をもって物事を鑑賞し、それを楽しむことが「風流」なことで、そうした行為を日本人は洗練されたものと感じるのです。

　「風流」を体得し、それを実践できる人は「風流人」と呼ばれ、文化人として尊敬を集めます。

　「風流」とは風の流れと書きますが、その表記の通り、風が流れるようにさりげなく、心地よく日本の伝統美を表現できる人こそが「風流人」であるといえるのです。

　そうした意味では「風流」は「粋」にも通じる概念で、それは日本人があこがれる感性であり、ライフスタイルです。

　もちろん、「風流」な人は美意識が洗練されているだけでなく、「徳」がある教養人となります。すなわち、日本人がよしとする価値観を体得し、それを美的なセンスをもって優雅に表現できる人が「風流」な人なのです。

Cultured

In the autumn there is an event called *tsukimi. Chūshū no meigetsu* refers to the beauty of a full moon viewed on a clear autumn night; it also refers to the event itself of admiring the moon in such fashion. The Japanese call the experience of appreciating such a sense of beauty *fūryū.*

Observing things with the Japanese sense of beauty, as described in this chapter, and enjoying that experience is *fūryū.* The Japanese consider such behavior to be very refined.

One who understands the true meaning of *fūryū* and who is able to put it into practice is called a *fūryūjin* and is respected as a person of culture.

The Chinese characters for *fūryū* mean "flow with the wind," and indeed a true *fūryūjin* is one who, like the movement of the wind, is able to express his appreciation of traditional Japanese beauty in a seemingly effortless way.

In this sense, *fūryū* is closely related to the concept of *iki* ("chic"). Both of these qualities are much admired by the Japanese.

It is true of course that a *fūryūjin* is not only a person with a refined sense of beauty; he must also be an educated person of principle. In other words, a *fūryūjin* is a person who has a strong grasp of the basic values and aesthetic sensibilities of the Japanese and who is able to express those values in an elegant and refined way.

□月見 moon viewing
□中秋の名月 Harvest moon
□ひんやりとした cool
□満月 full moon
□〜を愛でる admire
□章 chapter
□風流人 person of elegance and refinement
□表記の通り as stated
□さりげなく casually
□心地よく pleasantly
□感性 quality
□教養人 educated person
□優雅に elegant and refined

14

流

ながれ

Drifting Away

融通
ゆうずう

　例えば、人がお金を借りたとき、「あの人に**融通してもらった**」といいます。それは、貸した人がお金を必要な借主のために、心を開いて**柔軟に対応**したことを**暗に示しています**。ということで、この言葉は昔から金銭に関わる言葉として使用されることが多かったのですが、そこにはもう一つの隠れた意味がありました。

　あの人は**融通のきく人**だと言えば、**物分かりいい人**だということを示していたのです。つまり、融通とは**柔軟性**をも意味した言葉だったのです。その反対に法律や決まり事に従って、柔軟性なく決まった通りにしか物事を進められないことを**杓子定規な人**といって、人々はその対応を嫌いました。

　その昔、日本では杓子定規ではなく、相手の状況や心情、さらに背景や置かれている立場などを理解して、例え法律上は問題があっても情で物事を判断し、社会をうまく進めてゆこうという考え方がありました。それが、融通という価値観だったのです。融通は硬い制度と、**人情**の間に立って、社会をうまく進める**潤滑油の役割**を示した価値観だったのです。

　しかし、最近になって、こうした発想が社会での**公平な判断**に**支障をきたす**ということから批判されるようになったのです。そして、賄賂や特定の人への利益を優先させることを**戒め**、より公正な社会を目指す中で、融通という考え方はむしろ避けられるようになってしまいました。しかし、そのことで、社会の中の**潤**いがなくなり、潤滑油によってちょっと調整をしようという判断ができにくくなっているのも事実です。融通という考え方のプラスの部分が失われるなか、世の中はだんだん**世知辛く**、人の心への配慮が少なくなってきていると思っている人が多いのも事実です。

Accommodating

As an example, when someone loans us money, we may say, "She accommodated me." This is a tacit indication that the person who loaned money to the borrower was kind and flexible. In the past, this expression was most frequently used in connection with financial help, but there was another, less apparent meaning involved.

To say that a person was accommodating or flexible implied that the person was understanding. That is, accommodating also conveyed the meaning of flexibility. The opposite was someone who was strict and inflexible, who followed laws and regulations and who was rule-obsessed, the type of person that most people found to be incompatible.

In ancient times, Japan was not obsessed with rules. It was felt that society would progress best by taking into account the other person's situation and feelings, the background and the position in which the other person was placed. Even in the case of something that had to do with laws, decisions would be made by taking feelings into account. This was the value of "accommodation." This flexibility stood between strict systems and human emotions and was the sense of values that functioned to reduce friction, to smooth things out, so that society could operate smoothly.

However, in recent times this way of thinking has come under criticism in society as bring about obstacles to unbiased decision-making. With an eye to creating a just and impartial society which prohibits bribery and grants priority that benefits certain people, the idea of accommodation has fallen out of favor. However, as a result, at the same time social leeway and warmth has decreased, and in fact the smooth relations that previously allowed slight adjustments are no longer present in the making of decisions. As the positive elements in the concept of accommodation have disappeared, many feel that the world has gradually become a harder place to live and consideration of the feelings of others has decreased.

☐ 融通する accommodate

☐ 借主 borrower

☐ 柔軟に flexibly

☐ 暗に示す imply

☐ 金銭 cash

☐ 融通のきく accommodating or flexible

☐ 物分かりいい understanding

☐ 柔軟性 flexibility

☐ 杓子定規な rule-obsessed

☐ 人情 human emotions

☐ 潤滑油 lubricating oil

☐ 公平な判断 unbiased decision-making

☐ 支障をきたす hinder

☐ 賄賂 bribery

☐ 戒める prohibit

☐ 潤い enrichment

☐ 世知辛く become a harder place to live

忖度
そんたく

　忖度とは、人の心を推し量って判断したり、時には扶助したりする考え方を指す言葉です。もともと融通と共に、忖度はそれほどマイナスの意味を持った言葉ではありませんでした。

　しかし、近年、政治の世界で仲間うちの利権や権力の維持のためにこの発想が使われてきたことが社会問題になって以来、忖度はどちらかというと否定的な価値観と捉えられようになりました。

　どんな価値にもプラスの部分とマイナスの部分があることは誰でも知っていることでしょう。しかし、そのマイナスの部分が強調され過ぎた時、その価値観自体が糾弾され、壊されてしまうこともあるのです。

　例えば、「あの人にはお世話になったから、あの人の子どもに苦労をさせたくない」と言って、大学の入学試験の時に特別にその子どもの入学を許可すれば、それは公私混同で違法行為にすらなってしまいます。その時、忖度してしまったと言って糾弾された人は、社会に対して謝罪するわけです。しかし、お世話になった人の子どもに良いことをしてあげようという行為は、伝統的には、恩に対して報いるという日本の前向きな価値観だったのです。しかし、それを社会の制度を曲げて運用するときに、忖度の負の部分が出てくるわけです。

　今、日本では、伝統的な価値観の負の部分が削除される中で、人々の心持ち自体に変化がおきています。日本人が古来持っていたアイデンティティが失われることへの危機感を持っている人も多くいるはずです。忖度という価値観のプラスの部分を育ててゆくにはどうしたらいいのかは難しい課題です。教育や社会を通して人と人との関わり方そのものへの探究が必要です。是は是、非は非としながら、昔からの潤いある社会をどう維持してゆくか。今ちょうど日本人にはそうした課題が突き付けられているのかもしれません。

Intuiting the Unspoken

The term *sontaku* indicates the making of a decision by surmising someone's feelings and sometimes providing assistance that is unrequested. Initially, along with *yūzū*, the word did not carry a significantly negative nuance.

However, in recent years, this way of thinking has become socially problematic because it has been sued as a means of preserving vested interests and power among political circles. As a result, *sontaku* has come to be seen as a rather negative social value.

Most people surely grasp the fact that every social value has both positive and negative aspects. However, when the negative aspect is overly emphasized, that value itself is denounced and the whole value is done away with.

For example, consider a case where someone who is in a position of authority at a university has been kindly treated by another person and thinks, 'He has done so much for me in the past that I would not want his child to suffer in any way.' When the child is taking an entrance exam to that particular university, the first person wants to arrange to have the child specially admitted. This would be an instance of mixing public and private matters that could even become a matter of illegal activity. In this case, the person denounced for *sontaku* then has to apologize to society for his actions. However, from the traditional perspective, the person who was attempting to do something that would benefit the child of the person he was indebted to was motivated by the Japanese positive value of repaying an obligation. However, when that personal sense of value is put to practice in tweaking the social system, the negative aspect of *sontaku* comes to the forefront.

In present-day Japan, as the negative parts of traditional values are being eliminated, people's frame of mind is changing. Many Japanese may sense an impending crisis at losing their long-held identity as Japanese. How one is to deal with the positive aspects of *sontaku*, which have been cultivated in society, has become problematic. It is necessary to examine the way in which people interact with one another through education and society. While approving right and condemning wrong, should one maintain the means of reducing friction that have been passed down through the ages? Japanese may well be confronting this type of issue today.

□推し量って surmising
□扶助する assist
□利権 vested interests
□糾弾される be denounced
□公私混同 mixing public and private matters
□恩に対して報いる repaying an obligation
□削除される eliminated
□是は是、非は非 right is right, wrong is wrong

癒し（いやし）

　世の中が、融通がききにくく、お互いへの配慮や思いやりに基づいた忖度がしにくくなれば、当然人々は**心の余裕**を失ってゆきます。近年、世界経済の中で日本が**低迷**し、**所得**が増えず、心にも余裕がなくなっている中で、人々の心の中に癒しという**価値観**を大切にすることが多くなりました。

　癒しとは、自然の中で疲れた**心身**を**治癒**したり、人間関係が緊張する中で、優しい言葉を掛け合ったり、時にはふと一人になって好きなことに**没頭**することで、心の痛みを回復することを意味しています。そして今、人によっては、日本の伝統的な価値観などへも目を向けて、失われつつある**古き良きものへの郷愁**にひたることに癒しを求めようともしています。

　秋に京都に紅葉を見に行ったり、江戸時代をテーマにした人と人との心のやり取りを描いた映画を観たり、伝統工芸に没頭したりという行為が90年代から現在まで、日本人の中に多く見られるようになりました。社会に余裕がなくなった分だけ癒しへの**執着**が深くなってきたのです。そして、さらにその**延長**には、今までただがむしゃらに組織のために働いてきたことへの反省も見られるようになったのです。仕事より自分や家族の癒しを大切にした価値観が認められるようになったのです。

　個人を大切にしようという考え方は、そのまま**終身雇用**などの伝統的な日本社会のあり方に**疑問を投げかけ**、制度そのものの見直しにも繋がるようになりました。癒しを求め、過去に当然だとされた価値観が見直されているにもかかわらず、その行為の向こうにちらほらと見えるのが、実は失われつつある日本人の伝統的な事柄への**憧れ**であるのは、考えてみれば不思議なことだといえそうです。

Peace of Mind

As the world around us becomes less accommodating (*yūzū*) and there is less intuiting of unspoken desires (*sontaku*), people naturally lose a degree of peace of mind. In recent years, amidst Japan's economic slump, in which there is no increase in wages and there is little peace of mind or emotional leeway, many people have been placing a high value on *iyashi*, emotional healing.

Iyashi refers to any number of things. It includes psychological and physical healing in natural settings, someone speaking kindly in the midst of stressful human interactions, occasionally becoming completely immersed in a favorite activity—anything that promotes healing and recovery from emotional stress. Some people now seek this kind of healing by immersing themselves in the nostalgia for traditional Japanese values.

One can see this in the number of people who travel to Kyoto to see the changing colors of autumn leaves, who watch movies depicting the Edo period and the human relations of that time in history, and who, since the beginning of the 1990s, have become devoted to traditional crafts. To fill the gap left by the diminished leeway within society, people have become obsessed with attaining *iyashi*. And as a sort of extension of this, one observes a variety of soul-searching vis-à-vis what has been a habit of working energetically for some organization. There is more recognition of placing less emphasis on work than on increasing one's own peace of mind and that of one's family members.

The idea of placing emphasis on the individual has cast doubts on what has been taken to be standard Japanese society, including the notion of lifetime employment, and has led to a reexamination of the system as a whole. In searching for *iyashi*, not only have the values of years gone by been reexamined, but one can find here and there a degree of reverence for the Japanese traditions that have been lost. When one thinks about this, it is quite a remarkable phenomenon.

□ 心の余裕 peace of mind
□ 低迷する slump
□ 所得 income
□ 心身 body and mind
□ 治癒する heal
□ 没頭する immersed
□ 古き良きもの the good old things
□ 郷愁 nostalgia
□ 心のやり取り heart-to-heart exchanges
□ 延長 extension
□ 終身雇用 lifetime employment
□ 疑問を投げかける cast doubts
□ 憧れ reverence

ゆとり

　ゆとりとは、**余裕**のあることを意味する言葉です。そして現代人はこの言葉を金銭的な余裕よりも心の余裕を意味する言葉として使うようになりました。

　日本人は戦後の**荒廃**から**立ち直る**ために、昼夜をおいて働き、社会を発展させました。その世代が高度成長期の日本を作り、その子どもたちはその恩恵によって**バブル期**の繁栄を謳歌しました。当時は会社や社会の繁栄を第一として、人々は仕事に没頭したのです。そしてバブルが弾け、さらにバブル世代の人々が親になり、その子どもである現在の若者が育ってゆきます。

　今を生きる若者の多くは、それまでの価値観に**懐疑的**です。むしろ成功しなくても、金銭的に豊かさを求めなくても、**それなりの幸福**の中で静かに生きることを求めます。それが今を生きる人々のゆとりという価値観です。教育の上でも、それまでの**進学**重視の詰め込み教育を否定した「ゆとり教育」という制度も一時ありました。この教育を受けた人々をゆとり教育世代といいます。彼らやその後に育った若者は、終身雇用という価値観も持たず、個人の生活を大切にします。そんな**達観**した感情を「悟り」と呼ぶ人もいるのです。それは、先に紹介した修行によって**会得する**悟りとは異なる新たな価値観といえましょう。

　そんな若者を**自尊心**や**自己達成感**がないと昔を生きた人々は批判します。それがまさに日本流のジェネレーションギャップなのです。しかし、バブル**崩壊**以降、日本経済は低迷し、世界の中での相対的な地位も**揺らい**でいます。その影響で、貧富の差や教育の**格差**が社会問題となり、日本社会は決してゆとりのあるものではなくなりました。であればこそ、若者の抱くゆとりや悟りといった価値観の向こうに何が見えてくるのか。今後の日本社会にどのような影響を与えるのか。それはまだ**未知**の**領域**なのです。

Leeway

Yutori has the meaning of leeway, ease, and a degree of latitude. To present-day Japanese, *yutori* refers less to financial leeway than to psychological ease.

In order to recover from the destruction of World War II, the Japanese people had to work day and night to rebuild their society. That generation created the period of high economic growth. Their children celebrated the benefits and blessings in the period that became known as the economic bubble. The strongest images that remain of that period are companies and employees totally absorbed in working hard. When the bubble burst, the young generation had already become parents. In turn, their own children are today's youth.

Many of today's young people are skeptical of the values that have continue to the present. Rather than struggling to succeed, they prefer not to seek financial affluence but rather to pursue a life of reasonable happiness. Their values seek to live a of ease in the present. In the realm of education, there was a period in which *yutori kyōiku*—education with a degree of leeway—rejected education that aimed at cramming in order to pass harsh entrance exams to elite schools and universities. Students who received their education during this period are known today as the *yutori kyōiku* generation. Neither that generation nor the one that followed hold to the values of life-long employment. They place emphasis on personal life. Some people refer to this far-sighted view as *satori*, enlightenment or higher perception. This is the deep understanding attained by discipline, which has been described elsewhere in this book, and one can call it an entirely new sense of values.

People in the past would be critical of these young people's lack of pride and self-respect and their lack of any sense of accomplishment. Beyond doubt this is a Japanese version of a generation gap. However, since the burst of the economic bubble, the Japanese economy has slumped and Japan's international economic ranking has been undermined. As a result, the gap between wealth and poverty and the gap in education have become social problems. Japanese society has certainly not become more relaxed. That being the case, what is the outlook beyond the *yutori* that young people embrace and the values of the *satori* generation? What kind of influence will they have on Japanese society from this point onward? This remains unknown territory.

□ 余裕 allowance, leeway, room

□ 荒廃 devastation

□ 立ち直る recover

□ 高度成長期 the period of high economic growth

□ バブル期 bubble period

□ 謳歌する celebrate

□ 懐疑的 skeptical

□ それなりの幸福 reasonable happiness

□ 進学 entering a higher-level school

□ 詰め込み教育 cramming

□ 達観 far-sighted view

□ 会得する attain

□ 自尊心 pride and self-respect

□ 自己達成感 sense of one's own accomplishment

□ 崩壊 collapse

□ 揺らいでいる shaky

□ 格差 gap

□ 未知の領域 unknown territory

191

忍
にん

75

　この言葉は、世界中で人気を博した忍者の「忍」に他なりません。

　忍は「しのぶ」とも読みます。それは目立たず、辛いことにも耐えて、自分の役割を全うすることをよしとする価値観です。もちろんこの価値観は本書で紹介した、謙遜や修練、求道などという価値観に通じる日本人の心の持ち方に深く関わります。

　しかし、面白いことに21世紀になってゆとりや悟りが云々される中で、忍は「諦め」という言葉に置き換えられたように思えます。古い価値観の影響を強く受ける年配者と、その人たちが作った社会とのギャップの中で若者が悟るとき、過去の価値観に強い反発を持って行動するのではなく、変わらない社会への「諦め」、つまり現代流の諦観を持ってしまうのです。それが、物言わぬ現代を生きる人々の「忍」の姿かも知れません。

　悟りも忍も、昔は僧侶や武士が修行の中で培い、日本人の価値観の根本を形成しました。しかし、そんな価値観が変化した現代の癒しの世界では、それはノスタルジックな古き良き時代の価値観だと思われています。黙って文句を言わず、忍ぶことが求道の精神だと思われていた昔と違い、今人々は強い自己主張はしないものの、サラリと転職し、集団のニーズより自分の思いを優先させてゆきます。忍ではなく、黙ってその場から自分の姿を消してゆくわけです。

　とはいえ、現代を生きる人は言葉で主張はしないまでも、こうした行動によって立派に自己主張をしているのだと評価する意見がないわけではありません。

　忍という価値観が、そうした新しい日本人の未来にどのように馴染んでゆくのか、興味あるところです。

Patience and Self-Restraint

The Japanese character *nin* is, obviously, the base of the word *ninja*, which has gained worldwide popularity.

Nin is also read as *shinobu*, which means to conceal the self, endure hardships, and willingly fulfill one's role. This value has of course been introduced elsewhere in this volume, and it is deeply embedded in the Japanese values of modesty (*kenson*), self-discipline (*shūren*), and seeking after truth (*gudō*).

Interesting enough, however, in the 21st century in connection with *yutori* and *satori*, *nin* has become a variety of replacement term for resignation (*akirame*). In the gap between themselves and the older generation which was strongly affected by the older values and the society those values created, the younger generation has achieved a certain awakening or enlightenment which has led them to strongly rebel against the older values. Instead, they have resigned themselves to surviving in a society that does not change. In a sense, they have adopted a contemporary variety of philosophical endurance or resignation. It may be seen as an unspoken form of self-restraint (*nin*).

In the past, Buddhist priests and samurai cultivated *satori* and *nin* through ascetic practices and these molded the fundamental values of the Japanese people. However, in the present, where society embraces *iyashi*, those values are seen as nostalgic remnants of the good old days. As opposed to the past, in which remaining silent without complaining and simply enduring, which was seen as the correct path in the search for truth, although the current generations do not strongly assert themselves, they place priority less on salary and career moves and place more on their own feelings. Instead of endurance, they silently disappear from the scene.

Having said that, even though Japanese in the present day do not express themselves verbally, one can say that they are successfully expressing themselves through their actions.

It will be quite interesting to see how this value of *nin* will permeate the Japanese people in new ways in the years to come.

□ 人気を博した which has gained popularity
□ 目立たず inconspicuously
□ 耐える endure
□ 役割を全うする fulfilling one's role
□ ～が云々される中で amidst discussion of
□ 諦め resignation
□ ～に置き換えられる be replaced by
□ 年配者 elderly person
□ 反発 rebellion against
□ 僧侶 Buddhist priest
□ 古き良き時代 good old days
□ 黙って silently
□ 自己主張する assert oneself
□ サラリと without hesitation
□ 集団のニーズ group needs
□ 馴染んでゆく permeate

同調圧力

76

日本社会はもともと狩猟社会ではなく農耕社会でした。**個人芸が重んじられ**る狩猟社会と比較すると、農耕社会では**個人の権利や実力**以上に、村の中でどのように協力して秋の収穫を享受するかに人々は注力してきました。しかも日本は**島国**でしたから、**大陸国家のような大量の移民や他部族の侵入**による生**存競争**とも無縁の社会を長い間維持してきました。そんな遺伝子を引き継ぎながら、それでも現代社会では若い世代を中心に、自分の実力を相手に示し、自らのニーズをしっかりと主張することが良いことだという**観念も浸透**しつつあります。そこには海外からの影響もあるでしょう。

しかし、欧米社会などと比較すれば、日本人は他者の目を気にします。多数の人がある行動をとることを当然とすると、その発想に逆らってあえて自己主張をすることは回避しがちです。そんな見えない社会の圧力を同調圧力と呼んでいます。コロナ感染症が流行したとき、**法的に規制されていなくても**、誰もが同じようにマスクをしました。アメリカなどでマスクをしない人々の強い意思が表明されたとき、多くの日本人は欧米流の**個人主義的な**考え方に戸惑いを抱いたはずです。

この同調圧力は、海外からみると**社会規範を重視する礼儀正しい日本人**の姿として映ったかもしれません。しかし、日本社会をみるならば、こうした同調圧力の末に社会全体が**全体主義**に傾きながら、戦争へと向かっていった過去があることを忘れてはなりません。**堂々と物をいうことをはばむ**見えない圧力は、人への**配慮**というプラスの面と、ダイナミックで多様な社会を創造しにくいというマイナスの面があるわけです。日本人にとってこのマイナスの面をいかに克服するかは、21世紀の世界の中で激しい競争を生きぬくための大きな課題でもあるのです。

Pressure to Conform

In its origin, Japanese society was not a hunting culture, but rather an agricultural society. In contrast with hunting societies in which individual skill was considered important, in agricultural societies, cooperation with the village and enjoying the benefits of a shared autumn harvest were more important than individual rights. Moreover, because Japan was an island country, it survived for a long period without the struggle for existence experienced by continental peoples who faced large numbers of immigrants and different tribes. Although it inherited this tradition, present-day society—centered around the young generation—widely shares a sense that it is acceptable to directly exhibit their own abilities to others and to express their own needs. It is likely that this is due to influence from overseas.

However, in contrast with Western societies, the Japanese still remain quite concerned about how others view them. When, as a matter of course, it becomes necessary for a large number of people to take action, the Japanese avoid expressing themselves in a way that could be taken as going against the group's fundamental idea. This invisible social pressure is the pressure to conform. During the Covid pandemic, even when there were no legal regulations requiring the wearing of masks, people wore them because everyone else did. Observing countries like America, where some people strongly resisted the wearing of masks, many Japanese must have been puzzled by the insistence upon such an individualistic way of thinking.

From outside the country, the pressure to conform may have seemed like the social model emphasized by polite Japanese. However, when one examines Japanese society, this pressure to conform can turn into totalitarianism, which one cannot forget led Japan into war in the past. The power to invisibly impede speaking out has, on the one hand, a positive impact in emphasizing consideration of others. On the other hand, however, there is a negative aspect that makes it difficult to create a diverse society. For the Japanese, how one can suppress this negative aspect will be a major challenge in attempting to survive the harsh competition of the 21st century.

- ☐ 個人芸 individual skill
- ☐ 個人の権利 individual rights
- ☐ ～を享受する enjoying the benefits of
- ☐ 注力する focus on
- ☐ 島国 island country
- ☐ 大陸国家 continental country
- ☐ 移民 immigrant
- ☐ 他部族 other tribes
- ☐ 侵入 invasion
- ☐ 生存競争 struggle for existence
- ☐ 無縁の unrelated
- ☐ 実力 abilities
- ☐ 観念 notion
- ☐ 浸透する permeate
- ☐ 法的に規制されていない not legally regulated
- ☐ 個人主義的な individualistic
- ☐ 社会規範 social model
- ☐ 礼儀正しい polite
- ☐ 全体主義 totalitarianism
- ☐ 堂々と openly
- ☐ ～をはばむ prevent
- ☐ 配慮 consideration

沈思黙考
ちん　し　もっ　こう

　日本人が**沈黙**に強いことはすでに説明しました。沈思黙考は、じっと黙って思索に耽ることを示す言葉です。古来、そんな姿は賢人の典型的な行動様式だとされてきました。そして、日本人は言葉にすることなく、行動して結果を出し、さらにそのことは他者にアピールせずにいることに美学を覚えてきました。儒教の言葉に「巧言令色、鮮なし仁」という言葉があり（☞p.142）、美しい言葉で表現し過ぎることは、**誠意**のない証拠であると解釈されました。控えめで、静かで、それでいて深い教養のある人のことを、人々は「**奥ゆかしい人**」と言って称賛していたのです。それが日本人独特の**不言実行**という価値観の原点となりました。

　とはいえ、昔に比べ、日本人ははるかに自己表現をするようになりました。スポーツ選手などが、勝利した時に**ガッツポーズ**をして全身で喜びを表現したりする行動も、最近では当たり前になってきています。会議などで目を閉じて黙って考えている姿は、**陳腐化した古いタイプ**の日本人を示すステレオタイプとなっているかもしれません。また、「奥ゆかしい」という言葉に**至っては**今ではほとんど使われなくなってしまいました。

　しかし、それでも日本人は、しっかりと声をあげて自己主張をすることはやはり**稀**なのです。あの同調圧力というベクトルが働けばなおさらです。沈思黙考や不言実行の美学は古いものとされながら、逆に自分の考えや思いを**理路整然**と雄弁に語ることは、やはり**言い訳がましい軽率な行動**と取られかねないのです。

　伝統的な価値観が**形骸化**し、ただその行動様式だけが受けつがれるとき、社会は**停滞**してしまいます。今、そんな形骸化が**危惧されている**のがここに紹介した沈思黙考や不言実行の美学なのかもしれません。

Lost in Contemplation

As explained elsewhere in this volume, Japanese are especially comfortable with silence (*chinmoku*). *Chinshi mokkō* refers to being silent and absorbed in thought. In ancient times, this was the mark of a truly wise person, a sage. Among Japanese, it was considered a high principle to show results through actions rather than words, and to do so with no intention of appealing to others. There is a Confucian saying to the effect that "He who gives you fair words feeds you with an empty spoon," meaning that elegant phrases alone are not honest proof of sincerity. If a person is reserved, soft-spoken, and has a deep understanding of learning, people would refer to the person as a "modest person." This fundamental principle was at the base of the essential Japanese distrust of mere words and deep trust in actual deeds.

Having said that, in comparison with the past, Japanese have become much more self-expressive. It has recently become much more common for athletes when they win a competition to punch the air in triumph, expressing their joy with their whole body. The old stereotype of Japanese sitting silently in a meeting with their eyes closed may be obsolete. And the reference to someone being gracefully self-effacing may no longer be common.

However, it is still uncommon for Japanese to speak up, to express their thoughts. Even more potent is the force toward conformity. While the aesthetics of silent contemplation and dependence on actions rather than words belong to the past, the fluent and logically consistent expression of one's thoughts and feelings can still be taken as an indiscreet way of making excuses.

When traditional values turn into mere formalities and only the behavioral pattern is passed down, society grows stagnant. The apprehension that they may be turning into simple formalities may indicate the value of these concepts of *chinshi mokkō* and *fugen jikkō*.

□ 沈黙 silence
□ 思索に耽る be absorbed in thought
□ 誠意 sincerity
□ 控えめ reserved
□ 奥ゆかしい modest
□ 不言実行 action before words
□ 原点 point of origin
□ ガッツポーズをする punch the air
□ 陳腐化した obsolete
□ 〜に至っては especially when it comes to
□ 稀 uncommon
□ 理路整然と in a logical manner
□ 言い訳がましい seeming like a justification
□ 軽率な indiscreet
□ 形骸化 turning into mere formalities
□ 停滞する grow stagnant
□ 危惧されている concerned

洒脱と気っ風

　江戸っ子気質という言葉があります。江戸は東京の昔の名前です。

　18世紀末に100万都市にまで成長した江戸は、町人文化が栄えた活気ある街でした。江戸で快活に活動していた人々のことを江戸っ子といいます。彼らの間ではさっぱりした心意気が好まれました。ストレートで着飾らず、少々おせっかいなほど他人にも情に厚い人々がもてはやされたのです。そんな人のことを洒脱な人といい、彼らは気前もよく細かいことにあまりくよくよすることを嫌いました。多少見栄っ張りではあるものの、お金が入れば気前よく人に振る舞い、困っている人がいれば貸し借りを抜きにさまざまな扶助をします。そんな行為を「気っ風がいい」と人々はもてはやしました。

　日本の伝統的な美学といえば、今までに紹介したわびやさび、さらに幽玄といった伝統芸能にも通じたものが主流だと思われています。しかし、江戸時代以降、こうした気軽でユーモアや人情を重んじる人生の美学がもてはやされました。これは、身分が最も高いとされた武士ではなく、巷の町人の間で育まれ、明治以降も受け継がれた気質でした。

　とはいえ、今東京に昔ながらの江戸っ子がいるかといえば、それは稀になりました。現代社会では、そんな洒脱で気っ風のいい生き様を美学とすること自体が困難になっているのです。特に都市部では人と人との疎外が進み、アパートに暮らしていると隣の人が誰かもわかりません。見知らぬ人へのおせっかいは却って迷惑がられます。江戸が東京になって150年以上が経過した今、洒脱で気っ風のいいライフスタイルは物語の中の価値観となってしまったのです。

　現代社会は西欧文明が東洋のライフスタイルに変化を与えながらつくられました。その現象は日本でも同様で、そうした変化の中で失われつつある価値観の代表が、人と人とが人情で繋がる江戸時代の町人のものの考え方なのかもしれません。

Sophisticatedly Witty

There is a unique characteristic referred to as *Edokko* spirit, Edo being the old name for Tokyo.

By the end of the 18th century, Edo's population had grown to one million. The city was prosperous and filled with the culture of the townspeople. Among them, an open-hearted spirit was much admired. Straightforward, unrefined, slightly nosy about the affairs of other people, yet soft-hearted, the ethos of the townspeople was widely acclaimed. Such people were referred to as chic and sophisticatedly witty. They were generous and did not fret over small details. While they might have been somewhat ostentatious or pretentious, when they had money, they generously entertained others. When someone was in need, they willingly offered money and other forms of support. Such actions were made much of as examples of open-heartedness.

Speaking of traditional Japanese aesthetics, we have elsewhere introduced *wabi* (a taste for the simple and quiet), *sabi* (subdued refinement), and *yūgen* (the subtle and profound) that is thought to permeate traditional performance arts. However, since the Edo period, the aesthetics of light-hearted humor and warm-hearted lifestyle became broadly popular. This aesthetic was not that of the high-status samurai class, but emerged in the quarters where the townspeople lived, and it was passed on following the Meiji period.

Although there is something of the *Edokko* remaining in Tokyo, it is rare. In present-day society, it is hard to support such an urbane, witty lifestyle as an aesthetic today. Especially in urban areas, people have become more and more alienated from one another and people living in apartments don't even know who their neighbors are. Sticking one's nose in other people's business is simply annoying and no longer acceptable. Edo became Tokyo more than 150 years ago, and the sophisticated, urbane character of the *Edokko* lifestyle is a sense of value found only in theaters today.

Contemporary society was formed from the impact of Western civilization on Eastern lifestyles. The phenomenon was the same in Japan. Representative of what was lost in this process might well be that open-minded, warm-hearted relationship between townspeople during the Edo period.

- ☐ 気質 temperament
- ☐ 100万都市 city of over a million people
- ☐ 快活に cheerfully
- ☐ さっぱりした心意気 openhearted spirit
- ☐ ストレートで straightforward
- ☐ 着飾らない plain, casual
- ☐ おせっかいな nosy
- ☐ 情に厚い soft-hearted
- ☐ もてはやされる widely acclaimed
- ☐ 洒脱な chic and sophisticatedly witty
- ☐ 気前がよい generous
- ☐ 見栄っ張り ostentatious or pretentious
- ☐ 人に振る舞う treat someone
- ☐ 扶助 support
- ☐ 気っ風がいい open-heartedness
- ☐ 幽玄 subtle and profound
- ☐ 巷の in the public
- ☐ 疎外 alienation
- ☐ 現象 phenomenon

やばい

　つい最近まで、「やばい」という言葉は何か危険な状態にあったり、まずいことをしてしまったりしたときに使う表現でした。つまり、「やばいよ」といえば、深刻で困ったぞという意味のスラングだったのです。

　しかし、最近特に若者は感動したり、自分の感情や情熱がプラス方向に盛り上がったりしたときにやばいと言います。年配者は最初こうした言葉の変化に戸惑い、違和感を感じました。しかし、言葉は時と共に変化するのです。

　やばいという言葉を今を生きる人が使うとき、その背景には日本語自体への意識の変化がうかがえます。実は、昔は感動し、高揚感を覚えたときにはさまざまな表現がありました。しかし、現在、誰もがこうした多様な表現を一つにまとめて「やばい」という言葉で語ってしまいます。時には単に楽しい思いをした時にも「やばい」という言葉を使います。こうした言語感の変化は、バブルが弾けた頃から顕著になりました。例えば、「とても」とか、「非常に」という極端な状況を表現するときに、若者がそれらをすべてまとめて「超」という言葉を使い始めたのも90年代以降のことでした。試験を受けて「超難しかった」といえば、「手に負えないほど困難なことだった」ということになります。

　確かに言葉は時代によって変わってゆきます。現在江戸時代の武士の言葉を使う人は誰もいません。しかし、日本語の中の繊細な意味合いや感触を「やばい」という一言で片付けてしまう世代が増えていることに、言葉の現象だけではない、日本人の価値観の変化を感じている人も多いのではないでしょうか。

Super

Until quite recently, the adjective *yabai* was used to refer to dangerous, risky situations and it was applied to things that were awkward and disadvantageous. In other words, when someone described something as *yabai*, it was a slang way of describing serious trouble.

Nowadays, however, particularly young people use the term when they are impressed, in a positive sense to express their feelings or excitement. Older people were at first bewildered by that meaning and somewhat uncomfortable about how it was used. However, words change with the times.

When people today use words like *yabai*, they become aware that the background of the Japanese language is changing. In the past, when people felt excitement or an upsurge of emotion, there were various ways of expressing it. Now, however, people use a single word like *yabai* to express all of these feelings. On some occasions *yabai* is used to express joy or delight. This change in the view of language was particularly striking when the economic bubble burst. For example, *totemo* (very) and *hijōni* (really) came into use to express an extreme condition. Young people in the 1990s began combining both of those meanings into one word: *chō*, meaning "super" or "ultra." In explaining an exam as *chō-muzukashii* (ultra-hard) they meant that it was completely beyond their ability to pass.

To be sure, vocabulary changes with the times. No one uses the language of the Edo period samurai any more. However, in the fact that the subtle nuances and connotations of Japanese are reduced to a single word by people in one generation after another suggests that one can find change not only in language but also in the values of Japanese as well.

□違和感 sense of discomfort
□言葉は時と共に変化する words change with the times
□高揚感 upsurge of emotion
□顕著になる become noticeable
□超 super or ultra
□確かに be sure
□繊細な subtle
□意味合い nuance
□〔言葉が持つ〕感触 connotation

映える

　スマートフォンで風景を撮影し、それをインスタグラムに**アップする**ことは、誰もがやっていることでしょう。アップしたくなるような素敵な風景のことを、人々は「**インスタ映え**」すると表現します。早春の朝の**膨らみかけた桜の蕾**や、夏陽に輝く花畑など、インスタグラムで人が「いいね」をしそうの風景を「インスタ映え」というのです。

> 「春は 曙 (夜明けどき)、
>
> 　夏は夜、
>
> 　　秋は夕暮れ、
>
> 　　　冬は早朝」

　これは11世紀の**清少納言**による**随筆**「**枕草紙**」の冒頭の文章の一部です。そこではそれぞれの四季の中でどの時間帯が好きかを作者は語ります。**今流にい**えば、彼女にとってのインスタ映えを感じるときのことを**綴った**ものといえます。もともと「**映える**」とは、時の流れの中で、目に止まる**鮮やかな美しさ**を意味しています。それは瞬時のことが多く、その直後には風景は移ろいます。

　元来、日本人は自然の変化の中に、世の中の**無常**を重ねてみるセンチメンタリズムを和歌や俳句、さらに詩や随筆の中に記してきました。現代人がそれをインスタグラムによって追いかけるのは、癒しの追求の延長かもしれません。枕草紙が執筆された平安時代から現在まで、「映える」ものへの**感傷**、そして「**映える**」ものが移ろうことからくる無常観などが日本人の心の奥底に受け継がれてきました。典型が「**夕映え**」という言葉です。それは夕陽が沈む直前に自然が放つ鮮やかな風景を指しています。

Looking Attractive

Almost everyone today takes photos with their smartphones and uploads them to platforms like Instagram. People search for beautiful scenes and take photos of them, referring to them as "Instagrammable." In early spring mornings, they take photos of cherry blossoms beginning to bloom and in summer sunshine they do the same with fields of brilliant flowers. Any scene that might attract "likes" from viewers is "Instagrammable."

> Spring at daybreak
> Summer at night
> Autumn at dusk
> Winter at the break of day

This is from the opening passage of the eleventh century random musings titled "The Pillow Book" written by Sei Shōnagon. The author includes her favorite time of day in each of the seasons. In modern terms, it can be said that she sets down the parts of the days that are Instagrammable. Originally the term *haeru*, appearing attractive, carried the meaning of something of graceful beauty that catches the eye within the flow of time. In many cases, it lasts just an instant, and immediately afterward the scene fades.

Originally, the Japanese attempted to capture within the changes of seasons in nature the impermanence of the world and portray it in *waka*, *haiku*, poems, and miscellaneous writings. In today's Instagram images, people may be pursuing a similar kind of peace of mind (*iyashi*). The sentiments that are recorded in "The Pillow Book" during the Heian period and are still sought today may indicate that in the depths of the minds of the Japanese there is an inherited consciousness of the mutability of the world. A classic example of this is the word *yūbae*, evening glow. It refers to the dazzling natural color that the sun gives off just before it sets on the horizon.

□ アップする upload
□ インスタ映え Instagrammable
□ 膨らみかけた beginning to swell
□ 蕾 bud
□ 夏陽 summer sun
□ 曙 daybreak
□ 清少納言 Sei Shōnagon (c. 966-1017 or 1025)
□ 随筆 random musings
□ 枕草子 The Pillow Book
□ 今流にいえば in today's terms
□ 綴った spelled out in writing
□ 鮮やかな美しさ graceful beauty
□ 無常 impermanence
□ 感傷 sentiments
□ 夕映え evening glow

世界中のどこの国にも独自で美しく特殊な文化があり、日本もそんな世界の仲間の一つです。日本は山の多い島国で、四季があり、文明が育まれた日本の数少ない平地や盆地は照葉樹林帯に属していました。そんな背景の中で、大陸とも交流しながら日本人は独自の文化を育み、世代から世代へとつないできました。「映える」ことへの日本人の執着は、そんな日本人を取り巻く自然環境と、そこに持ち込まれた仏教観などが関わって培われました。

　こうした日本人の感性は伝統的な芸術やアニメなどの現代アートに反映され、世界の人々から注目されました。「映える」ことは、平安時代からコンピューター世代に至る日本人の心を象徴する価値観だといえそうです。

Every country has its own unique, distinctive culture, Japan among them. Japan is an island country with many mountains, four distinct seasons, and a culture that was created in its numerous flatlands and valleys surrounded by evergreen broad-leafed forests. Against this background, while Japan carried on exchanges with the continent, the Japanese created their own culture and one generation passed it on to the next. Japanese people's attachment to *baeru* was nourished by the natural environment that surrounded them as well as the Buddhist views that were brought in from the continent.

Such Japanese sensibility is reflected in the traditional arts, anime, and other forms, and these attract the attention of people around the world. The notion of *baeru*, showing things to advantage, is a sense of value that symbolizes the spirit of the Japanese—from the Heian period to the computer era.

□照葉樹林帯 evergreen broad-leaved forest zone

□仏教観 Buddhist worldview

□感性 emotional sensitivity

Read Real NIHONGO

日本人のこころ
Heart & Soul of the Japanese

2024年1月6日　第1刷発行

著　者　山久瀬　洋二

訳　者　マイケル・クーニー

発行者　浦　晋亮

発行所　IBCパブリッシング株式会社
　　　　〒162-0804 東京都新宿区中里町29番3号　菱秀神楽坂ビル
　　　　Tel. 03-3513-4511　Fax. 03-3513-4512
　　　　www.ibcpub.co.jp

印刷所　株式会社シナノパブリッシングプレス

© IBC Publishing, Inc. 2024

Printed in Japan

ISBN978-4-7946-0796-6